lucky
people

lucky people

a neuroscientist's guide to attracting luck, cultivating success and leading a happier life

nobuko nakano

GALLERY BOOKS UK

Copyright © Nobuko Nakano 2023. All rights reserved.
First published in Great Britain by Gallery Books, an imprint of Simon & Schuster UK Ltd, 2026
Original Japanese edition published as SHINPAN KAGAKU GA TSUKITOMETA "UN NO II HITO"
by Sunmark Publishing, Inc. in 2023.

English translation rights arranged with Sunmark Publishing, Inc. through Japan UNI Agency, Inc.
and Vicki Satlow of The Agency, srl

The right of Nobuko Nakano to be identified as the author of this work has been asserted in
accordance with the Copyright, Designs and Patents Act, 1988.

1 3 5 7 9 10 8 6 4 2

Simon & Schuster UK Ltd
1st Floor
222 Gray's Inn Road
London WC1X 8HB

For more than 100 years, Simon & Schuster has championed authors and the stories they create.
By respecting the copyright of an author's intellectual property, you enable Simon & Schuster
and the author to continue publishing exceptional books for years to come. We thank you for
supporting the author's copyright by purchasing an authorised edition of this book.

No amount of this book may be reproduced or stored in any format, nor may it be uploaded to any
website, database, language-learning model, or other repository, retrieval, or artificial intelligence
system without express permission. All rights reserved. Enquiries may be directed to Simon &
Schuster, 222 Gray's Inn Road, London WC1X 8HB or RightsMailbox@simonandschuster.co.uk

www.simonandschuster.co.uk
www.simonandschuster.com.au
www.simonandschuster.co.in

Simon & Schuster Australia, Sydney
Simon & Schuster India, New Delhi

The authorised representative in the EEA is Simon & Schuster Netherlands BV, Herculesplein 96,
3584 AA Utrecht, Netherlands. info@simonandschuster.nl

The author and publishers have made all reasonable efforts to contact copyright-holders for
permission, and apologise for any omissions or errors in the form of credits given. Corrections may
be made to future printings.

Simon & Schuster strongly believes in freedom of expression and stands against censorship
in all its forms. For more information, visit BooksBelong.com.

A CIP catalogue record for this book is available from the British Library

Hardback ISBN: 978-1-3985-5118-3
Trade Paperback ISBN: 978-1-3985-5119-0
eBook ISBN: 978-1-3985-5120-6

Typeset in Parango by Envy Design Ltd

Printed and Bound in the UK using 100% Renewable Electricity at CPI Group (UK) Ltd

Contents

Prologue: What Kind of Person Is Lucky? 1

1 Lucky People Put Themselves at the Centre of the World 15
2 Lucky People Are Convinced of Their Own Luck 53
3 Lucky People Try to Live in Harmony with Others 89
4 Lucky People Set Their Own Standards for Happiness 127
5 Lucky People Pray 155

Epilogue: Lucky People Cultivate a Lucky Brain 175

References 181
About the Author 185

Prologue

What Kind of Person Is Lucky?

Have you ever noticed that some people seem to be inexplicably lucky? Things always seem to go their way, and when you see them, you can't help thinking, *there goes a lucky person*. In a corner of our minds, we are always conscious of luck. Perhaps you are out driving and the lights stay green, so you think, *Lucky!* Or at the supermarket checkout, maybe only your queue is moving and so you feel a little bit lucky. Or perhaps you feel lucky about winning a fantastic prize in a contest, but at the same time a little bit uneasy about 'using up' your luck. And there may be times when you think, *if only I were lucky*.

Maybe you believe that luck – good and bad – is something that cannot be changed, and that those of us who are not blessed with good luck can do nothing about it. But I would challenge the idea that how lucky we are is beyond our control. Take Kōnosuke Matsushita, founder of Matsushita Electric Housewares Manufacturing Works, the company that became today's global Panasonic corporation. Matsushita is known as 'the God of Management' in Japan, and he might also be considered one of the luckiest people in the country: a self-made man without wealth or connections, he succeeded in turning a small factory into a major international company.

Whenever Matsushita held hiring and recruitment tests, he always finished with the same question – 'Are you a lucky person?' – and only hired those who had answered yes, because he considered people who believed themselves lucky were less likely to give up or become dispirited in the face of adversity. Instead, he thought, their belief in themselves and confidence that everything would be all right equipped them to deal with any problem head on and overcome it. He understood luck not to be preordained or something we are born

What Kind of Person Is Lucky?

with, but determined by the individual's mindset and patterns of behaviour. In his view, the fact that lucky people share certain mindsets and behavioural patterns meant that luck is something we can control. And if those mindsets and behavioural patterns are conducive to good luck, it should be possible to improve your luck by making them habitual: you should be able to train your brain to attract luck.

This book is based on the idea that luck can be cultivated. I am an independent scholar and neuroscientist. I studied neurology at the University of Tokyo Graduate School of Medicine, and continued my research at the Saclay Nuclear Research Centre in France until 2010. Luck is seemingly unscientific and perhaps an unlikely subject for a scientist, but I have drawn on my training in neuroscience to identify the mindset, patterns of behaviour and conduct that are conducive to becoming lucky, giving us pointers for cultivating a 'lucky brain'. I believe that close scrutiny of science can shed light on things that at first glance may appear unscientific, and can reveal unexpected and hidden scientific depths.

Lucky people often say things such as: 'It's good to

say out loud, "I'm lucky! I'm blessed",' or 'Write your dreams, goals and desires down on paper, pin it up, and they will come true,' and 'Be grateful to other people.' These claims are usually based on personal experience and have almost no scientific basis. Nonetheless, these people have good luck. Why is this? How do we become lucky? What kind of person has luck on their side? In this book I take a scientific approach to address these questions.

Survival of the Luckiest

What do we consider as being lucky? Is it someone who is financially well-off or doing work they love? Perhaps it's someone who is living a healthy, long life or who is sharing their life with the person they love? Is it someone who does as they please? Everyone has their own take on what constitutes luck, but, from a scientific viewpoint, a key word is 'survival'.

Charles Darwin was influenced by the concept of survival of the fittest in developing his theory of evolution, the idea that organisms best adapted to an environment will survive. The giraffe's neck is a famous

How do we become lucky? What kind of person has luck on their side? In this book I take a scientific approach to address these questions.

Lucky People

example of this: animals with longer necks can see further and protect themselves from enemies, as well as eat leaves from tall trees more easily, and so giraffes with long necks are the result of the environment they live in. Survival of the luckiest, however, is quite different. This concept – from the neutral theory of molecular evolution – is simply that the lucky survive, and so the giraffes that were lucky enough to survive just happened to have long necks.

The exact reason for giraffes having long necks is still not understood. If it were due to survival of the fittest, there ought to be evidence of their necks having gradually developed in length, yet no fossil record of any interim stage has ever been found. Nevertheless, survival of the fittest still seems the most plausible explanation.

How can the case of ocean sunfish be explained, then? This fish lays 270 million eggs at a time, of which only one or two survive to reproduce. In terms of survival of the fittest, the one surviving fish would be deemed more suited to the environment than the other 269,999,999 eggs, whereas survival of the luckiest would have it that the one surviving fish is luckier than

What Kind of Person Is Lucky?

the rest. It seems both unlikely and unnatural that only one or two out of so many eggs could be genetically suited to survival; good luck seems a more plausible explanation for the survival of the one fish. Yet if we consider this phenomenon from a macro perspective – survival of the entire species over very long periods of time – the best explanation is still survival of the fittest, whereas over shorter periods (such as a human lifetime) or in a population with a relatively small number of individuals, the principle of survival of the lucky generally applies.

The thought that only the lucky survive and ultimately there is nothing to be done about it can be quite dismaying. The one ocean sunfish egg that survives does so because of numerous instances of luck: it did not encounter an enemy; it was able to protect itself from the enemies it did encounter; it did not lack for food. This makes it sound as if luck is like destiny and is beyond control; each individual egg has innate predetermined luck, and only those with the best luck survive. It may appear as if that egg has no active involvement with its own luck.

Is this the same for humans? Is there no hope of

changing our luck through trying, and do we have no choice but to submit to it? I do not believe so. I believe that luck – good and bad – is random and impartial, but that we can at least be proactive in making the most of it.

The Random Nature of Luck

Let's examine why luck happens, using a numerical theory called the random walk model. If a coin is tossed and it comes up heads, you move one step forward, but if it shows tails, you go back one step. What happens if the coin is tossed 10,000 times and the results plotted on an axis of co-ordinates? The end result will almost never see you standing on exactly zero; most of the time, you will end up 200 to 300 steps forward or back from zero. Similarly, it almost never happens that the 10,000 tosses result in all heads (a forward step) or all tails (a step back).

The same can be said of luck. The random walk model helps illustrate why some people feel they have been constantly lucky, or constantly unlucky, in the past. We may think good luck and bad luck occur in

What Kind of Person Is Lucky?

roughly equal measure over the course of our lives, but if we view life like a random walk, we see that the odds always lean one way or the other to a certain degree over the limited period of a lifespan. There are so few people for whom it is overwhelmingly negative or positive as to be almost non-existent.

From a neuroscientific perspective, people characteristically perceive a period of prolonged negative results as bad luck, and consecutive positive results as good luck. To our brains, a run of five positive results feels too much to be random, even though it is. A continuous sequence of either good or bad events can go on longer than that, but our brains find it difficult to accept as nothing more than coincidence. Conscious attempts at rational review fail to dispel the impression of bias one way or the other. This kind of mistaken reasoning is called a 'fallacy'.

In the well-known Münsterberg illusion, slightly staggered black and white squares are sandwiched between the parallel horizontal lines, making them appear sloped. It is impossible to perceive them otherwise. The same mechanism at work in optical illusions also influences the brain in its observation of events

Lucky People

that occur in our lives. In other words, luck depends on the brain's perception of it as good or bad, and analysis based purely on appearances may be nothing more than illusion.

How We Perceive Luck

Countless instances of good luck and bad happen all around us, but we remain unaware of them. Say, for example, someone dropped an envelope stuffed with one million yen (£5,000) in cash on the street where you always walk to work. That particular day, you happened to wake up early and decided to vary your route, getting off the train one stop early to get some more exercise in. If you had gone your usual way, you might have found the envelope, taken it to the police station, and later claimed the money if the owner didn't

What Kind of Person Is Lucky?

appear. You did not have that good fortune, however, because you went a different route, though you remain unaware of this.

In another scenario, had you gone your usual route, you might have had the misfortune to run into someone you did not want to see, tripped over a stone and fallen. But you are unaware of having dodged this piece of bad luck because you went a different way. We tend to notice only visible fortune and misfortune, labelling it good luck or bad, yet in reality we are all subject to innumerable instances of good or bad fortune to which we remain oblivious.

Why is it, then, that some people appear to be lucky and others unlucky? Broadly speaking, it is because lucky people have the ability to capitalise on a greater share of the good luck that falls equally to everyone, to deflect more of the bad luck, and to turn bad luck into good. Unlucky people are the opposite: good luck slips easily away from them, they hold on to bad luck and are unable to turn it around into good. If you look closely at people often called lucky, you will notice common patterns of behaviour, mindsets and ways of thinking. In other words, lucky people are not simply blessed

> *Lucky people have the ability to capitalise on a greater share of the good luck that falls equally to everyone.*

What Kind of Person Is Lucky?

with good fortune; they are the ones who make a grab for it, deflecting bad luck through their conduct and thinking. How does this work? Why are they able to create good luck and prevent bad?

This is akin to our perception of happiness: we are inclined to believe that people who have money are happier, when in fact it might be more accurate to say that happy people make money. Indeed, a team of researchers at the University of Florida reported that happy people tend to have more money-making opportunities. A similar relationship could be said to exist between luck and the behavioural patterns and thinking of lucky people. For example, people said to be lucky will value and look after themselves in many ways. They treat themselves with care and adhere to their own values without being unduly influenced by others or general opinion. They are also far more considerate than average of other people, are not always looking out for themselves, and instead try to live in harmony with other people. Generally speaking, they live well. You could say that luck is on their side *because* they live good lives.

Surprisingly, many behavioural and thought patterns shared by lucky people can be explained by science. The same is true for saying 'I am lucky' out loud, or why pinning up paper with hopes, goals and dreams written on it can lead to them coming true, as well as why it is good to be appreciative of others. This book introduces the scientific evidence for the concrete actions and mindset that will enable you to improve your luck, such as 'put yourself at the centre of the world', 'convince yourself you are lucky', and 'try to live in harmony with others'. I will draw on my knowledge of neuroscience to throw light on why these strategies work, and suggest actions to take or ideas that you can immediately start implementing to improve your luck. The explanations I offer are based on scientific evidence, and not simply experience or hearsay. I hope you will find them convincing and motivating.

Putting these strategies and actions into practice can lead to a better way of life. A slight change to your usual mindset or behaviour may not result in a sudden change of luck for the better, but the cumulative effect of daily effort will lead to each day being a little better than the one before. Then, before you know it, the way you live your life will have changed, and with that, luck will be on your side.

Chapter One

Lucky People Put Themselves at the Centre of the World

Lucky People Make the Most of Who They Are

When you are envious of someone else's good fortune, you might try to change yourself to become like that person. If you consider financially well-off people to be lucky, you might endeavour to become financially well-off yourself. Those of us who consider a long and healthy life to be the sign of a lucky person might make more effort to be healthy. Whether it's wealth, health or another aspect of someone's life that makes us consider them lucky, we often strive to become like them by changing ourselves or our environment through study or other means.

Yet, although trying to change yourself to become lucky may at first glance appear to bring you closer to your goal, I believe it could be counterproductive. This is due to the nature of the brain. Each person's brain has its own characteristics, largely responsible for forming our individuality, and these are very difficult to change.

Neurotransmitters such as serotonin, dopamine and noradrenaline – the chemical messengers that influence our emotions and motivation – vary in amount from person to person. Serotonin works to reduce excessive arousal and activity in the brain, bringing a sense of security, stability and calm. Dopamine is the source of drive, working to raise our motivation when we go to do something. Noradrenaline heightens concentration, among other functions. They are all essential for our health, but in excess they can have an adverse impact on the brain and body. For this reason, our neurons also contain an enzyme called monoamine oxidase that breaks down serotonin, dopamine and noradrenaline, regulating the overall amounts in our body. Genetic individual differences in the degree of decomposition caused by this enzyme are one factor in making each brain unique.

Women who have a low level of degradation by monoamine oxidase are thought to experience happiness more easily and have a high innate sense of happiness. People with particularly low levels are said to experience high levels of happiness and be prone to such dissocial

Lucky People Put Themselves at the Centre of the World

behaviour as compensated dating (dating for financial rewards or gifts). In men, a low decomposition rate of monoamine oxidase is said to be associated with aggressiveness.

It initially seems contradictory that a natural-born sense of happiness should lead to a propensity for antisocial behaviour, but a low decomposition rate of monoamine oxidase means high volumes of serotonin are secreted, reducing anxiety. Anxiety stems from the ability to think ahead, envision and consider the future; without anxiety, we cannot not think about the future. In other words, if levels of serotonin secretion are too high, people are more likely to engage in antisocial behaviour because they find it enough to be satisfied with the present moment and do not think ahead.

These are just some examples of the innate individual traits of our brains. While inescapable, they can to a certain degree be controlled through self-awareness; if you recognise your own individual traits, you can try to regulate them. For instance, if you know that you don't like thinking too far ahead, you can undertake to consciously think about the future once a day. However, we cannot completely change our brain's individuality and, though we may try to become a version of the person we think is lucky, the bottom line is that it is extremely difficult to change yourself.

Let's consider this from another angle, then. Instead of trying to change yourself, you can try to make the most of the person you already are. For example, the flip side to antisocial behaviour born out of a heightened sense of well-being is being fearless. Fearless personalities can make the most of their personality in professions such as sales or those involving large financial transactions, or they may be able to offer encouragement to those with a sense of insecurity. Aggressive types can demonstrate their abilities in professions that require verbal jousting, such as the law, or serving in PR or liaison positions within an organisation. If you look to make the most of the traits particular to your temperament – the positive ones as well as those that might initially appear a liability – you can strive to be in control of it all.

Even when your own personal circumstances are not quite in sync with the general status quo, if you accept your situation you can seek to make the most of it. For instance, if you find it difficult to attend school or to

"Let's consider this from another angle, then. Instead of trying to change yourself, you can try to make the most of the person you already are."

work in an office, think about what your difficulty makes you able to do instead of forcing yourself to fit into that environment. There is no need to conform to the norm; the most important thing is to be yourself.

I believe that an absolute requirement for becoming a lucky person is making the most of the whole sum of who you are now: your body, your thoughts, your values and your instincts. So, ask yourself how you can make the best of yourself as you are now. It is not about learning or acquiring new skills, but making the most of what you already have. This is one shortcut to becoming a lucky person.

Lucky People Treat Themselves Well

Treating yourself well is an extension of making the most of you who are, and something that I am sure all lucky people put into practice. For example, say you put your sock on in the morning and notice a small hole in it. A lucky person does not think, *'I won't be taking my shoes off today, so I'll just leave them on,* they change their socks. Or, when eating alone, a lucky person does not settle for fast food but instead takes themselves

Lucky People Put Themselves at the Centre of the World

somewhere that serves proper cooking, or makes it themselves, however simple. In short, don't be inconsiderate towards yourself. As a lucky person does, you should treat yourself well and with the same respect that you show to others.

I once read a book about the manners of the upper class that struck a chord with me. It was written by Nadine de Rothschild, who had been an actress at a small theatre in Paris and married into the French branch of the Rothschild family. She was born into poverty and left home at fourteen to work, finding jobs at places like a print shop and car factory. Eventually she became an actress, but she was never a major star or a beauty of great note. However, she met and married Baron Edmond de Rothschild, one of the richest men in the world, and became part of a world of beauty and luxury that was beyond anything she had ever imagined. She is a woman who brought luck on to her side. In her book she wrote that the first thing to be mindful of is yourself: if you live alone, you should always keep your home clean and tidy; if you drink tea alone, you should use your finest cup, not something with a chipped edge; if you are eating alone at home, you should buy yourself

Lucky People

flowers and a delicious dessert on the way home. In other words, you should be attentive to yourself so that you come to like yourself and treat yourself well. You must care for yourself.

As I was reading this, I found myself nodding in agreement. It confirmed what I believe: people who treat themselves well create opportunities for themselves. But why does treating oneself well lead to being lucky? A person's luck is largely influenced by how well they build relationships with those around them. People who are considerate of themselves will be treated similarly by others, whereas people who are careless of themselves end up also being treated that way by others.

Say there are two cars in front of you. One is polished sparkling clean and the other is dirty, with bumps and scrape marks on the body. If you were told to hit one of the two cars hard with a stick, which would you choose? Most people would choose the dirty car because – as shown with the 'broken windows' theory (the idea that small misdemeanours can give rise to more serious crimes) – where there is already disorder, people are less psychologically resistant to adding to

Lucky People Put Themselves at the Centre of the World

that disorder. For example, you would feel ashamed to drop anything on a perfectly litter-free street, but feel it might be OK to drop one piece of rubbish on the side of a street already strewn with litter.

This same impulse happens with people: if someone cares for themselves we are resistant to treating them poorly, whereas if someone treats themselves without care, we feel it is acceptable to also treat them poorly. Similarly, you might instinctively use respectful language towards someone who is well dressed but feel resistant to showing that same respect to someone who is careless about their appearance.

In other words, to be treated well by others and build good relationships with people around you, you must first treat yourself well. In the words of Nadine de Rothschild, be mindful of yourself so that you can like yourself.

Lucky People Have Their Own Measure for Happiness

Lucky people always have their own standards of happiness, understanding which situations work for

"In other words, to be treated well by others and build good relationships with people around you, you must first treat yourself well."

Lucky People Put Themselves at the Centre of the World

them and make them comfortable. Having your own standard of happiness means knowing what makes you happy.

This varies from person to person. Some people's happiest time might be relaxing in a cafe and reading a book. Some people find happiness in having a clean, tidy home. There are those who like spending time with their dog, while others get their greatest enjoyment from playing sport. Some people may even be most happy when they are at work or studying. Whatever the source of your happiness, in order to bring luck on to your side, you must decide it in accordance with your own values and the criteria that matter to you rather than being swayed by general opinion or others' values. As we saw, Nadine de Rothschild suggests drinking from your best cup and not an old chipped one, even when drinking tea alone. But if that old chipped cup happens to be a present from someone dear to you, you have used it for many years and drinking from it is always a pleasure, then it is fine to keep using it for ever. Nadine de Rothschild might be adamant that, even in this scenario, she would still not use the chipped cup, but it is up to the individual to make the choice. What matters is that you properly assess how you feel about it deep down, how your brain reacts, and then act accordingly. You should do what feels right and comfortable for you, not base your choice on what others might think.

Lucky people proactively strive to create situations that make them feel comfortable and good, in accordance with their own criteria. This leads to luck because having an individual measure for happiness also has the power to attract people.

People who actively strive to produce situations that make them feel comfortable and good are constantly stimulating a circuit inside the human brain called the pleasure reward system. Located relatively deep in the brain, this is the general term for the parts involved in producing the sensation of pleasure, and includes the lateral hypothalamus, the thalamus, the medial forebrain bundle, the ventral midbrain, and the caudate nucleus. When these areas of the brain are stimulated, we feel pleasure – not only from our instinctive desires, such as appetites for food or sex, but also from social actions that produce a good feeling, such as helping someone. People who actively strive to produce situations that

Lucky People Put Themselves at the Centre of the World

make them feel good are constantly stimulating this reward system. Another way of looking at it is that people who can skilfully manipulate their own reward system are able to find satisfaction with their current situation.

When people are in a state of being truly comfortable, they feel the greatest happiness, forgetting about all other desires, only conscious of how pleasant and good it feels right now. In that moment they may even feel they want for nothing else. If we can create a state of contentment – if we stimulate the reward system – we can achieve what is called in psychological terms a congruence of self. This state of self-congruence is achieved when the ideals for the self are in alignment with the actual self, and you can accept yourself in that moment as you are. Simply put, you like yourself. You don't feel you need to be smarter, better at work, thinner and so on, but rather are able to admit to yourself that you are fine with yourself, just the way you are.

There is absolutely nothing aggressive about people in a state of self-congruence; they are very easy to be with since they are always in a state of contentment and other people are attracted to them. Being in their

Lucky People

presence makes others feel pleasure. They are able to listen with an open mind. Even when the other person is agitated, they have the capacity to absorb this. There is no reason for them not to be liked by others. In other words:

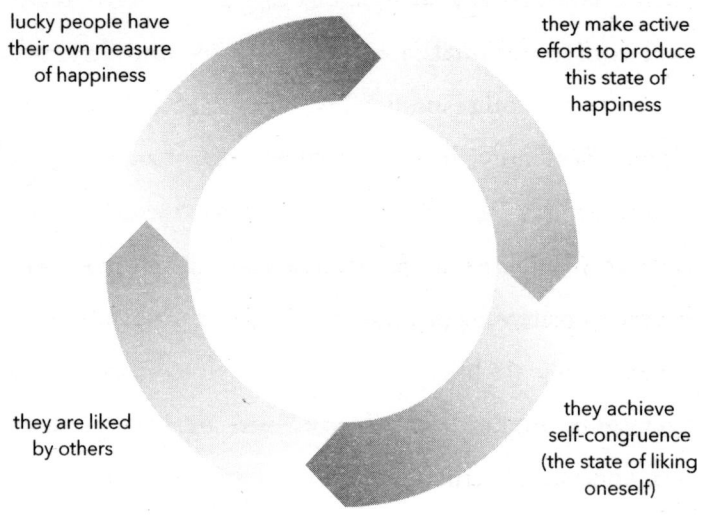

lucky people have their own measure of happiness

they make active efforts to produce this state of happiness

they are liked by others

they achieve self-congruence (the state of liking oneself)

Lucky People Question the Norm

Someone who is earnest, serious and hard-working, non-confrontational, listens dutifully and has a strong sense of responsibility might seem like a marvellous person to be around. Yet someone like this is an unlucky person in the making.

Lucky People Put Themselves at the Centre of the World

In Japan, some organisations are known as 'black companies' because their working conditions violate labour laws. The head of one such company spoke about his hiring policy in an interview, saying he always hired people who were 'easy to use' and that such characteristics included being serious and steady, non-confrontational, a dutiful listener, and having a strong sense of responsibility. Ordinarily, you would think these are admirable qualities, but when I read this interview I could see why a black company would take advantage of someone like this. Their qualities – deemed positive by ordinary standards of common sense – mean they are likely to be an unlucky person because they will unquestioningly conform to social norms. Someone who is trusting and obedient probably doesn't have a strong sense of self, which is the same thing as not valuing yourself. And when someone tends towards conformity, does not have a strong sense of self, and demonstrates a sense of responsibility, they will find it difficult to resign even when they realise there is something wrong with their new workplace and they do not feel comfortable there. They feel guilty about things like not being able to make good on their commitment and quitting while others around them are still trying. In short, they have a misplaced sense of responsibility.

Sometimes things considered 'good' according to common sense can have a negative impact if misused or wrongly applied. When we think about norms regarded as 'common sense' or 'common practice', we should not view them as absolute. Of course, there are many situations in which social rules and common sense should be observed, but we should remember that sometimes it is better for ourselves, and others, to act in accordance with our own judgement of a situation rather than simply doing as other people expect or say. It is important not to prioritise social rules and common sense above putting yourself first.

If you are someone who doesn't question social rules and norms, then you are what would be considered a low-level novelty seeker. Novelty-seeking is regarded as a genetically determined trait, varying in intensity from innately weak to middling to strong.

Say you go to buy a soft drink: do you automatically go for the same thing every time or do you tend to reach for the latest type or flavour? The latter indicates relatively strong novelty-seeking tendencies, and the

Lucky People Put Themselves at the Centre of the World

former relatively weak tendencies. Another example could be electronic devices and mobile phones: people who immediately buy the latest devices or models as soon as they are released have a strong novelty-seeking tendency, while people who reluctantly or rarely do so have a relatively weak novelty-seeking tendency. Someone with a strong novelty-seeking personality is disposed towards dissatisfaction with the daily routine, always desiring new experiences and the emotional thrill this brings. Those with weaker novelty-seeking traits tend to adhere to social rules and norms once they have decided these are right and will not change. They are prone to prioritising others' value over their own.

It is impossible to change our innate level of novelty-seeking, but by becoming aware of our own personality type, we can, to some degree, modify our behaviour. For example, if you tend to always buy the same thing, you now know that you probably have weak novelty-seeking tendencies and so you can remind yourself to buy a different flavoured drink next time – or you can at least be aware that you often swallow social norms unquestioningly and so you can modify your behaviour to be careful about this.

Ask yourself now: what is your own propensity for novelty-seeking? If you sense it is weak, check that you are not prioritising social norms and general opinion over yourself.

Lucky People Are Relaxed About Life

'Relax, take it easy' might sound like unexpected advice for being lucky, but in fact it is another aspect of living a life built on taking care of yourself. The opposite of being relaxed is being serious and earnest. We have already looked at how being serious and earnest can have negative effects; now I would like to consider in more detail the merits of being relaxed.

I once saw an online video of a train operating on the Yamanote Line loop in Tokyo. The camera was set in the front car, filming the view from train driver's seat between Shinjuku and Shibuya stations on four trains with different departure times on that route. The screen was divided into four so that all four could be viewed simultaneously, and you could see the difference in each train's speed from the flow of scenery. The astonishing thing was that there was almost no difference between

" It is impossible to change our innate level of novelty-seeking, but by becoming aware of our own personality type, we can, to some degree, modify our behaviour."

their speeds, and when there was it was within a few seconds. The filmmaker rode the Yamanote Line for several days, and the fastest time it took to travel an entire circuit of the loop was 60 minutes and 10 seconds, while the slowest time was 60 minutes and 25 seconds – a difference of only 15 seconds.

When I watched this video with a French colleague, his reaction was to sigh and say, 'Crazy...' I understood why. When I worked in France, I commuted on the French rail system every day, which, by Japanese standards, operated very sloppily. Strikes were unbelievably frequent, trains would be cancelled for unknown reasons, and very often trains did not stop at scheduled stations. From a commuter's point of view, it was very inconvenient. But strikes can be quite nice if the trains not working means you are treated to a sudden holiday and can choose to use the day for your own benefit.

Japanese trains are a stark contrast to French trains. If Japanese trains can be said to be punctual (and serious), then French trains are – with apologies to French people – slack (and relaxed). Suppose we impose this contrast in trains on lifestyle. The French train style of

Lucky People Put Themselves at the Centre of the World

living leans much more towards taking care of oneself. Think about how this plays out when, for instance, it comes to doing overtime: people who are assiduous and always do overtime are serious about work, whereas a more relaxed person promptly goes home when the day's work is done, without caring what others think, and goes out for a drink with friends or a partner.

Most of the time, employers' preference will be for serious, hard-working people in the workplace. Serious employees feel bad about leaving before others, and stay on to do overtime simply because their boss and others are still working. They may give an impression of being serious, when in fact they are merely constrained by the values of others around them. Some companies still cling to the belief that those who work the longest hours are excellent. Anyone who gets caught up in this value system can lose sight of their own value judgement. They are killing themselves.

In fact, those who 'kill' themselves are often 'killed' by others as well. This is the root cause of the senseless overworking of employees at black companies. More relaxed employees, on the other hand, may be out of sync with the values of the company, but they act in accordance with their own values. They have their own agenda of things that they want to do. Since they are not 'killing' themselves, they are also not being 'killed' by others.

Something else to be said for the French railway approach to life is that it has an abundance of flexibility. French trains are inconvenient in many ways, but their lack of reliability also brings some conveniences: even when a door is about to shut, for example, the driver will open it for you if you ask him, and I have often seen trains wait for passengers who are running to catch them. Flexibility makes it possible to respond quickly to unanticipated situations, and more spontaneity allows for richer possibilities when dealing with unforeseen circumstances. A relaxed and easy-going person is also more tolerant of mistakes and departures from the norm in others.

Of course, this is not to deny the value of a steady and earnest attitude. The quality of being serious and earnest is a necessary and important element of living in harmony with others. However, I think it is important to ask yourself from time to time if you are neglecting yourself by using reliability as a front. Have you lost sight of your own values? Are you constrained by the values of society at large? And have you forgotten what it is you really want to do?

Lucky People Respect Their Own Preferences

Everyone has their own tastes and their favourite foods, colours, animals, people, and so on. Most of the time there is no clear reason for a particular preference; when asked why we like a particular food or colour, most of us will find it hard to give a specific reason. Usually we just know that we like something. These personal preferences may be hard to explain but they cannot be denied. It is important to respect them because in some situations they lead to making the correct choice when it is a question of survival.

When choosing a partner of the opposite sex, men tend to place more importance on appearance than women do. There are several interesting research papers about this, mainly by William D. Lassek and Steven J. C. Gaulin in the United States. In their study, male subjects were shown photographs of women with

"Have you lost sight of your own values? Are you constrained by the values of society at large? And have you forgotten what it is you really want to do?"

various body types – thin, medium and full-bodied – and asked to select which they found most attractive. The results showed the male preference was for women with a hip-to-waist ratio of between 1 to 0.6 and 1 to 0.7 (for example, a woman whose waist was 65cm and had hips measuring between 92 and 108cm). The study also tested the intelligence of the children of women with the preferred hip-to-waist ratios, compared to the children whose mothers' hip-to-waist ratios fell outside that range. The results showed that the average IQ of the children of women with the preferred ratios was higher than the children whose mothers' ratios was not in this range.

The reason for men's preference is thought to be related to body fat types. Fat that accumulates around the waist, hips and stomach is called omega-6 fatty acids, while fat that accumulates around the bottom and thighs is called omega-3 fatty acids. These two different types of fats have different qualities. Omega-3 fatty acids form the material of the myelin sheath, a fatty insulating layer in the brain and spinal cord, meaning the fat that clings to the buttocks and thighs is the same type of fat that makes the brain grow. According to the authors of the paper, men subconsciously recognise that women who have a great deal of omega-3 fatty acids and little belly fat – an indicator of health risks and ageing – have a higher probability of giving birth to intelligent children. The greater part of the human brain is made up of fat. Neurons in the brain are made up of a cell body with a cell nucleus and two types of projections extending from there: dendrites and axons. Axons are wrapped in the myelin sheath, which does not necessarily occur naturally at birth in all axon nerve cells; most is produced in a process called myelination as we grow. Myelination dramatically increases the speed of information transmission between cells, and is a crucial part of brain growth.

In contrast to men's emphasis on looks, women are believed to attach importance to memory when choosing a mate, specifically inconsistencies between words and actions. In particular, they react strongly to whether or not a man has kept his word – a quality that helps determine if the man can be relied upon to bring back food. This may seem calculating, but historically it was a necessary quality for survival, especially in the age of hunting.

Lucky People Put Themselves at the Centre of the World

There are always exceptions to research findings – especially when it comes to evaluating children's performances, which can be greatly influenced by other factors such as environment and not determined solely on the basis of the mother's hip-to-waist ratio – but this doesn't mean that subconscious preferences have no scientific basis at all. There must be other demonstrable subconscious preferences that have not yet been examined or proved but have been honed over time and become part of the strategy by which humans select a mate and ensure the survival of the human race. In other words, as we saw when discussing the importance of taking good care of yourself, it is important to value your personal preferences.

Lucky People Base Decisions on Fun

Next time you are trying to decide whether to do something or not, ask yourself if it is interesting or fun. When faced with choices, we tend to think in terms of right and wrong, but I recommend we also use interest as a criterion for decision-making. One reason for this is the health benefit: people are happier when they are doing something for pleasure, rather than half-heartedly out of a sense of obligation, and happiness is good for health.

In his book *Lifenuts: A Community-Based Blueprint for Individuals to Live Longer, Healthier, and Happier*, Robert F. Kroeger refers to a study in London conducted on 3,800 participants between the ages of 52 and 79 found that those with a subjective sense of well-being – the scientific term for happiness and life satisfaction – have a 35 per cent lower risk of death than those without (calculated after taking factors such as age and lifestyle into account). Subjects were asked questions to evaluate the level of their sense of well-being, with a follow-up survey conducted five years later. The results showed that, compared to a mortality rate of 3.6 per cent for the group with the highest level of subjective well-being, the mortality rate of the group with the lowest level was roughly double that, at 7.3 per cent.

Why do people with a high level of subjective well-being live longer? One explanation is the influence of well-being on the body's immunological system and, in particular, on the different immunity cell types that keep us healthy. These vary depending on a person's state of mind but are better balanced in people with higher levels of subjective well-being, satisfaction and sense of fulfilment. Conversely, in those without a subjective sense of well-being, the balance is upset and they become ill.

Natural killer cells (NK cells) are a type of white blood cell and they vary according to mental state. Suppose you have an infectious disease such as influenza. Contracting an infectious disease means your cells have been invaded and taken over by a virus that is using them to propagate itself. NK cells will kill cells infected by a virus. They also destroy malignant cancer cells. Human cells are produced every day, but copy errors inevitably occur and cells become cancerous. No matter how young or healthy a person is, anything from dozens to thousands of cancer cells are generated every day in the body. NK cells will destroy these malignant cells, and so people with normally functioning NK cells are less susceptible to cancer. However, it is not necessarily a good thing for the activation level of NK cells to be too high; a moderate level is the ideal state. Someone with a sense of subjective well-being can be said to be maintaining the proper level.

Our state of mind also influences another substance produced by the immune system: interleukin-6. Levels of this substance are an index of pain and inflammation, and is particularly elevated in rheumatoid arthritis patients. Such patients have been found to experience a decrease in interleukin-6 levels – and so a reduction of their pain and inflammation – after listening to comic performances and laughing a lot. Pain relief is very important to a living body. Not only is the sensation of pain unpleasant, but the resulting contraction of blood vessels and stiffening of muscles has an adverse effect on the condition of blood vessels, increasing the risk of deep-seated bleeding and infarction.

It is often said that illness starts with the mind, and all sorts of experiments and studies are beginning to reveal the extent the mind's influence can have on physical health, but we know it is beneficial to health to maintain a state of feeling happy for as long as is possible. Basing everyday decisions at least in part on whether something is interesting or fun is one effective way to do this.

Another reason to do this is the effect it has on motivation. As we saw earlier, when people find

Lucky People Put Themselves at the Centre of the World

something interesting or fun, it stimulates the reward system in their brain, triggering the production of dopamine, the chemical messenger that is the source of motivation. When we make choices, we are more motivated to do what is interesting rather than what is right. Since dopamine is addictive, once you start doing something and it goes well, it stimulates a feeling of wanting to do it more. Therefore, doing something because it is interesting makes us more motivated and so is more likely to produce better results.

It is good to be reminded of this because, although we cannot always prioritise the interesting or fun choice over the correct one, as people grow older they tend to forget and become less likely to do things for the sake of fun. According to a paper by Tetsuya Ohira, former professor at the University of Osaka Graduate School of Medicine, children laugh on average 300 times a day, while adults laugh only 17 times daily. Over the age of seventy, this drops to just twice a day.

How many times have you smiled today? Remember to use whether you find something fun or interesting as a criterion for making decisions, and you will increase the laughter in your life.

" When people find something interesting or fun, it stimulates the reward system in their brain, triggering the production of dopamine, the chemical messenger that is the source of motivation."

Lucky People Say 'I Love You' to Themselves

'Don't worry, I still love you as you are,' I sometimes tell myself. Especially when I'm feeling down about causing someone inconvenience or hurt due to my carelessness. A psychiatrist friend of mine recommends that his patients say this as part of their treatment. He noticed that people who came to see him did not cherish themselves and so, in an attempt to change that, he began asking them to tell themselves, 'xxx, I love you.' Even patients who were apparently very resistant at the start began to value themselves more after saying this repeatedly over time.

We saw earlier that all lucky people value themselves, and valuing yourself means taking care of yourself: paying attention to your appearance, making the effort to eat healthily, keeping your surroundings tidy, and so on. The bottom line, however, is self-love, because people who dislike themselves are unlikely to value or care for themselves. If you love yourself, you will treat yourself with care, so the most important thing is that you like yourself. That is why I sometimes say to myself, 'I love you, Nobuko.' It is imperative to be generous and completely on your own side when you do this, even when your faults are glaringly obvious. Tell yourself, 'Don't worry, I still love you as you are, xxx,' and accept yourself for who you are.

For example, recently I made a mistake with the time I was meeting a friend. She had sent me an email suggesting we meet at Shinjuku at 11 o'clock, which I mistakenly read as 1 o'clock. It was a huge blunder on my part as I ended up making her wait for two hours. My error was plain, but I said to myself nonetheless, 'You really screwed up, but I still love you, Nobuko.' I apologised with all sincerity to my friend, and reflected carefully on what had happened, promising myself I would be more careful in future when making appointments.

That said, you need to have another, merciful self in reserve and to show yourself forgiveness. It is good to reflect on your mistakes, but you should also be able to show yourself unlimited tolerance so that you do not become depressed or come to hate yourself. Tell yourself, 'I still love you, as you are, xxx.' This simple strategy is especially useful for people who tend to be hard on themselves and who lack confidence.

"It is good to reflect on your mistakes, but you should also be able to show yourself unlimited tolerance."

Chapter Two

Lucky People Are Convinced of Their Own Luck

Lucky People Assume They Are Lucky

Lucky people are convinced of their own luck: this is one secret to improving luck. It doesn't matter if you have no evidence or track record of being lucky; put all that aside and simply take it for granted that you are lucky.

I once saw the findings of a survey on intuition. Do you believe women are better than men at sensing when their partner is having an affair? The person who conducted this survey started from the assumption that women's intuition was superior to men's in this regard. When asked 'Do you think you have a good sense of intuition?', more women than men answered yes. However, when it came to detecting lies, the results showed that slightly more men than women saw through lies (the difference was only 1 per cent).

The experiment reveals the gap between our subjective and objective reading of how good our intuition is, showing that those who believe in their own good intuition had almost no basis for saying so.

The same can be said of luck: some people believe themselves to be lucky and some believe themselves to be unlucky, but there is very little clear evidence to support the people who believe themselves lucky. In other words, you can decide that from now on you will be lucky, with no evidence needed to back that up. Calling yourself lucky, without proof, brings actual improvements in luck. For example, imagine things don't go well at work and you fail to secure a contract. In this situation, someone who thinks of themselves as lucky will say, 'I didn't get the contract even though I'm lucky. Maybe I messed up in the preliminary groundwork. Or maybe I didn't do enough research.' In contrast, the person who believes themselves to be unlucky will say, 'I didn't get the contract after all that effort because I'm unlucky.' The first person admits to room for improvement; the second person does not. People who believe themselves to be lucky are more likely to try harder next time, therefore raising the likelihood of success, but that does not happen with those who believe themselves to be unlucky.

"You can decide that from now on you will be lucky, with no evidence needed to back that up. Calling yourself lucky, without proof, brings actual improvements in luck."

The realm of relationships can provide more examples. Those who believe they are lucky will tell themselves, 'I am with this person because I am lucky.' If there is a quarrel, they put it down to their own fault or shortcoming. Those who believe themselves to be unlucky, however, will say things like, 'I try so hard but my partner doesn't understand me. I was unlucky to choose such a person.' People who believe themselves to be lucky create opportunities to further strengthen relations with their partner, while people who believe in their own bad luck won't have this chance and will instead set themselves up for greater discord.

In reality, most of the time, people who believe themselves to be lucky encounter the same set of circumstances as people who consider themselves unlucky. It is only how they perceive and deal with those circumstances that is different. Yet, over the course of time, the differences in outcome are magnified. This is why you are better off calling yourself lucky even if there is no scientific basis for it.

Lucky People Have a Positive Self-Image

The other important factor that goes hand in hand with a belief that you are lucky is a positive self-image. Having a positive image of yourself whenever you are faced with some kind of challenge, such as taking exams or a sports match, will also have a positive effect on the outcome.

If you have been entrusted with a difficult and important project at work, this is the time to have a positive and successful self-image, with thoughts such as: *'I was successful last time, so 'I can do it again; 'I was entrusted with this difficult project because my efforts and the results have been recognised; 'I have passed difficult exams before and 'I can do it this time too.* Tell yourself that you are ideal for the job and there's no reason you can't do it. Your positive self-image doesn't need to be based on anything particular; groundless self-confidence is quite all right (within reason) as it will increase the chances of the project succeeding.

This was demonstrated in an experiment called the Mental Rotation Task, conducted in the US by Croizet et al. A mental rotation task is when subjects are shown a figure (sometimes flat, sometimes three-dimensional) and asked to select the identical shape from a list of five or six figures, all of which are rotated, so it is extremely difficult to pick out the same shape at a glance. In order to identify the original figure, the subject has to picture the original shape and mentally rotate it. Studies have found that men generally give faster and more accurate answers than women in these tests.

In this particular experiment, American college students were given a simple questionnaire to fill in before doing the mental rotation test. The questionnaire was in fact a key part of the experiment. When asked about gender in the questionnaire, 64 per cent of female students were able to give the correct response to the mental rotation task, compared to the male group. In contrast, when asked which college they attended, this percentage rose to 86 per cent of that for male students. The majority of test subjects attended famous, elite universities, and the experiment concluded that answering a question about their college in the questionnaire bolstered the subjects' self-image, which in turn had a favourable effect on results.

Having a positive image of yourself can directly

"When tackling any kind of challenging task or problem, you should try to reject any negative thoughts about yourself and focus instead on having a positive self-image."

impact on performance. Therefore, when tackling any kind of challenging task or problem, you should try to reject any negative thoughts about yourself and focus instead on having a positive self-image. In combination with the conviction of your own good luck, a positive self-image will lay the foundations for a cycle of favourable outcomes to occur: it becomes easier to succeed at new tasks and challenges, and success then confirms your sense of being lucky, boosting your self-image and making the next challenge that much easier.

Suppose, however, that you meet with failure in your next challenge. As we saw earlier, people who believe themselves lucky will take this as an opportunity to reflect. Their next effort will be born out of that and, if they succeed next time, they can then get themselves back into a positive cycle.

Lucky People Say 'I'm Lucky' Out Loud

Telling yourself to be convinced of your own luck is easy, but it might be difficult to put into practice if you have always considered yourself unlucky. This is where training can be beneficial.

Lucky People Are Convinced of Their Own Luck

Consider what a miracle it is that you even exist in the world. The life of a human being is formed from the meeting of a sperm and egg. Though it varies by individual, the number of sperm in a single ejaculation is estimated to be between one and four hundred million. After ejaculation, the sperm wait for an egg and proceed towards the ampulla of the fallopian tube, but only a few dozen to a few hundred actually make it there. Of those that do make it, roughly only one can be fertilised, but if fertilisation is successful there is still only a 75 per cent chance of the fertilised egg fastening on to the uterine wall and becoming implanted. If it does become implanted, a certain percentage still do not result in pregnancy. Even if they do, approximately 15 per cent of all pregnancies are believed to end in miscarriage. As you can see, each individual life is the result of immense good fortune: one sperm out of countless, meeting with an egg and then a baby being born. When you think of it like that, doesn't it seem miraculous that you exist?

This same miracle also extends to your father and mother, and to your four grandparents. Of course, your grandparents had parents too, so there is a long and uninterrupted line of life stretching back in an incremental number of miracles. If even just one of these miracles had not occurred, you would not exist. Does that not seem fortunate?

Telling yourself 'I'm lucky' out loud is often said to be beneficial for improving your luck, and I recommend this kind of training. When human beings try to memorise something, the hippocampus, located deep in the brain, is activated. Human memory is information sent from sensory organs such as sight, hearing and smell to the hippocampus, where it is consolidated and sorted for storing in either the short-term or long-term memory, or forgotten immediately. The more sensory organs are involved in sending this information, the easier it is to strengthen the memory and the longer it will remain. Saying 'I'm lucky' out loud rather than simply thinking it makes it easier for the idea that you are a lucky person to become fixed in your head, because the information is reinforced through activating neurons involved in storing long-term memory. The same applies to writing out statements such as *I'm lucky!* or *Fortune follows me!* and pinning them where they will be seen so as to activate your sense of sight.

Lucky People Are Convinced of Their Own Luck

I recommend doing any such training exercises for at least three weeks, as it is believed to take that long to form new circuits in the brain.

Lucky People Proactively Seek Out Other Lucky People

One way to train yourself to think you are lucky is to surround yourself with other people who are lucky. From a scientific point of view, individual luck – good or bad – is not inherent but determined by patterns of behaviour. If you are around lucky people, the way they behave rubs off on you, enabling you to behave in a similar way and attract luck.

Humans tend to be easily influenced by the people in their proximity. Hence the old saying that a man who was thinking about marriage should look first at the mother of a prospective bride. Regardless of genetic similarities, the bride would be greatly influenced by the person she spends most time with (i.e. her mother), and many things about her – from mindset and attitudes to the way in which her clogs wore out, so to speak – would be similar. Accordingly,

"From a scientific point of view, individual luck – good or bad – is not inherent but determined by patterns of behaviour."

a man could judge by the mother if her daughter was a suitable marriage candidate for him.

Family genetic influences aside, why is it that we come to resemble the people who are always in close proximity? Nerve cells in the brain called mirror neurons are believed to play a large part in this. Mirror neurons were discovered in a study on monkeys conducted in the 1990s by a group led by the Italian neurophysiologist Giacomo Rizzolatti. The mirror neuron – so called because you feel the actions of others as your own, as if in a mirror – is activated both when a person performs an action and when they observe others perform actions: they are activated not only when you grasp something with your own hand, for instance, but also when you see another person grasp something with their hand. They are particularly noted for their ability to understand and respond to the intentions and purposes of others' actions. For example, if a monkey is shown a human holding an apple, the monkey's mirror neurons respond more strongly when the human brings the apple to its mouth than when the human puts it on a plate.

Mirror neurons can read the background to an action, perceive its purpose and intent, and respond accordingly. This is evident when you see friends or family and know without being told that they are irritated, because you can sense it from their behaviour. Similarly, if they have good news or are scheming about something, you can also tell from their behaviour. This facility of mirror neurons is linked with the ability to comprehend others' feelings and have empathy. Their presence in our brains is believed to be a big part of why we are able to understand and identify with the joys and sorrows of others.

Knowing this, the merits of proactively associating with lucky people become clear. Spend as much time as you possibly can around lucky people, observing them carefully, and your mirror neurons will fire in the same way as theirs, exactly as if you are behaving like a lucky person. Eventually, the action and behaviour you observe will become your own, and you will start to mirror their behaviour. Your mindset and attitudes will also come to resemble theirs. If that happens, you will certainly start to believe you are lucky.

It does not matter that this is an illusion, because simply being convinced of your own luck will get you to the starting line for improving it.

Lucky People Are Early to Bed and Early to Rise

Many successful people are early risers. They might get up at four in the morning to make the most of the three hours before their family wakes, and turn in for the night at ten. Or they might rise by five in the morning and leave for work at six. By the time the workday starts at nine, they have already done a good amount and set the day off on a smooth track. You often hear successful people say something similar when discussing their habits, but I have never heard a success story that involves the person working like mad till late at night every day, sleeping in until the last possible moment in the morning, then racing into work.

From a neuroscientific viewpoint, being early to bed and early to rise makes sense. There are twenty-five neurotransmitter chemicals that have been clearly identified in the human body, some of which bring about feelings of security, peace and happiness. Serotonin – known as the happiness hormone for its mood-stabilising quality and the sense of ease it brings about – is one of these. You could also say it is essential for improving luck, but serotonin becomes more difficult to produce when leading an irregular life, so a life with a good routine of rising early and going to bed early is important.

Our bodies naturally become sleepy when night falls and wakeful when morning comes. The body temperature is lower in the morning and gradually rises over the course of the day through the night, then falls again in the morning. This 24-hour cyclical body clock is called the circadian rhythm, and is normally set for humans to be active during the day and sleep at night. The human circadian rhythm is also characterised by periodic fluctuations in the production of neurotransmitters, such as increased melatonin during sleep. Melatonin is an important hormone that ensures good-quality sleep and protects the body. It is useful for slowing ageing by breaking down reactive oxygen and strengthening antiviral action.

Melatonin is produced from serotonin in the pineal body of the brain, meaning it will decrease without the proper secretion of serotonin, which in turn is triggered by the retina sensing natural light in the morning. Fifteen hours after serotonin secretion starts, melatonin secretion begins. A daily lifestyle that adheres to the body's circadian rhythm is therefore important for maintaining sufficient production of serotonin and melatonin. This means rising early, being exposed to morning sunlight, and going to bed early.

Melatonin is made from the essential amino acid tryptophan. Essential amino acids cannot be produced in the body and must be sourced from food, so a diet containing sufficient tryptophan is also vital for the body to produce serotonin. Tryptophan is found in fish with red flesh (like tuna), meat and dairy products, and, since vitamin B6 is also necessary for the synthesis of serotonin, it is good to eat these in combination with foods that contain B6, such as garlic, red pepper and sesame.

Other factors for stimulating serotonin production include being in a relaxed state, such as when having a bath, and a moderate amount of exercise. In other words, a regular lifestyle of going to bed early, rising early, getting moderate amounts of exercise, and having long, relaxing baths is conducive to the production of serotonin. If you think that you haven't been too lucky recently, the quickest way to turn that around might be to start leading a more regular lifestyle.

"A daily lifestyle that adheres to the body's circadian rhythm is therefore important for maintaining sufficient production of serotonin and melatonin."

Lucky People Have Good Fantasies

How great would it be if so-and-so was in love with me too! If we were on a date we could go and see a movie, walk on the beach, or eat at a fancy Italian restaurant!

Such are the daydreams you might have about someone you have a crush on. This is another way of improving your luck.

Along with serotonin, dopamine is another neurotransmitter essential for boosting luck. We eat because we are hungry, we study hard in order to pass an exam or get into a particular school – there is always some motivating factor for our actions, and dopamine is involved with this motivation. The brain releases dopamine when it senses you feel joy at being praised or having some kind of win. Since dopamine produces feelings of desire and pleasure, it is known as the hormone that creates the will to live.

The most efficient way to trigger the release of dopamine is a good romance. When you fall in love, and that feeling is reciprocated, your heart beats faster. This pounding of the heart is proof that dopamine has been released. In reality, a love affair cannot be started at will – and an existing one may involve quarrels and betrayal, making it difficult to sustain a pounding heart in a good sense – so I recommend fantasising.

If there is someone you like who does not reciprocate your feelings, you could fantasise about things going well with that person. Or it could be about someone famous, like an actor or celebrity. The important thing is to have a fantasy that makes your heart beat faster.

A good fantasy doesn't even have to be about a romance with someone else. For example, sometimes you see some popular comedians on TV with intense expressions who exude energy and focus. People like that are likely to be incredibly self-assured, thinking of the millions of viewers on the other side of the TV camera all concentrating solely on them, laughing at their gags. I imagine those comedians are thinking, *'I'm amazing, 'I don't dislike myself*. A fantasy like that will stimulate the release of dopamine, further fuelling their motivation. It sets up a positive cycle in which the jokes and patter become even more polished.

A fantasy featuring yourself being successful can also be effective. Picture yourself at work, receiving cheers and plaudits from your colleagues over a job well

" The brain releases dopamine when it senses you feel joy at being praised or having some kind of win."

done. Or imagine a product you've been working on filling the shelves in shops with customers lined up to buy it. Even just thinking about such happy things can improve your mood.

Good fantasies cost nothing, you can have them anywhere, anytime, but the effect is huge.

Lucky People Are Caring of Others and Help Them Grow

Is there anyone in your circle of acquaintances who you are fond of, and is in a position of need in some way? There may be children and grandchildren, of course, but how about a younger colleague at work, or someone more junior from school or college? These are people you could nurture, improving your own skills in the process and, in turn, your luck.

Research by neuroscientists Dr Craig Kinsley from the University of Richmond in Virginia and Dr Kelly Lambert of Randolph-Macon College reveals the effects that doing this can have. Their experiments showed that learning and memory skills were dramatically higher in rats with experience of giving birth than in virgin rats.

Lucky People Are Convinced of Their Own Luck

They compared one group of female rats who had twice had experience of giving birth, raising and weaning litters, with a group of females the same age who had never mated. The rats were placed in a maze containing hidden food that they had to find. The mother rats were able to memorise the location of food in a much shorter time than virgin rats. The same experiment conducted with marmoset monkeys once again resulted in the group of mother monkeys finding the food more quickly. Put simply, rats and marmosets devoted to raising young had higher learning and memory skills than those without this experience.

These results may suggest that raising biological children is important for improving memory skills and learning, but that is not so. In another experiment conducted by Kinsley and Lambert, mother rats, virgin rats and foster-mother rats were all placed in a maze with hidden food. The rats were trained to memorise the route to the food by always hiding it in the same place. In this case, the foster mothers were virgin rats who had been placed in the same cage with baby rats to become accustomed to them. (Apparently some displayed typical maternal behaviour such as licking and grooming babies.) This time the mother rats again proved to be fastest at memorising the route to the food, but the foster rats came second by only a slim margin.

A similar experiment compared father marmosets with bachelor marmosets. Male marmosets actively participate in child-rearing, with females often giving birth to twins. In this experiment, father marmosets were able to memorise where the food was more quickly than bachelor marmosets. In short, the results showed that the experience of nurturing a child – whether as a foster or biological parent – led to heightened learning and memory skills, which begs the question: what kind of changes occurred in the brains of these rats and marmosets?

The role of the hormone oxytocin has been posited as one factor. Oxytocin functions to promote contractions for giving birth and the secretion of milk after giving birth. It is also believed to have a calming effect on emotions and behaviour, to strengthen mutual trust, and to make marital bonds and bonds between parents and children easier to form – a characteristic that has earned it the name of 'love hormone'.

A research group led by Kazuhito Tomizawa at

Lucky People Are Convinced of Their Own Luck

Okayama University conducted an experiment in which they injected oxytocin into the brain of a mouse that had never been pregnant and placed it in a maze with hidden food. The maze had eight routes, with food hidden in four of those. The results showed that the mice with the most oxytocin injected into their brains were better at memorising the food locations. When mice with experience of pregnancy were given an injection in the brain to inhibit oxytocin and also placed in the same maze, they showed a deterioration in memory skills. These results show that oxytocin improves learning and memory skills.

Oxytocin is a hormone secreted more readily in women but also present in men's bodies. Experiments have shown that when male marmosets are placed in a cage, the level of oxytocin secreted is higher in males with offspring in the cage with them than those in the cage alone.

As these test results show, nurturing with attachment – even if not related by blood – causes oxytocin to be produced and subsequently raises learning and memory skills. It follows, therefore, that the act of caring for somebody – not necessarily a child but someone at work or in the community – can stimulate oxytocin production in humans too.

The company Uniqlo offers a case example that would appear to support this. Uniqlo is known for hiring a high ratio of employees with disabilities. In Japan the mandatory proportion of disabled employees is set at 2.3 per cent (as of January 2023), but the actual proportion in Uniqlo as of 2021 was 4.6 per cent. Uniqlo actively began hiring people with disabilities in March 2001, reaching 6 per cent the following year. Once there were employees with disabilities in the workplace, the company began receiving feedback on improvements in service. Tadashi Yanai, the CEO, speculated in an interview that hiring employees with disabilities had fostered co-operative attitudes and a greater sense of consideration in the workplace at each branch. Presumably, branch managers in shops where improvements in service were noted took the lead in creating a caring, nurturing workplace. The effect would spread through the function of mirror neurons, and there would be an overall higher level of oxytocin produced in the different branches, which could be said to lead to better service.

Lucky People Are Convinced of Their Own Luck

You often hear mothers say that raising children has led to their own personal growth, and this is true, since raising another person leads to nurturing the self, regardless of whether or not the person is a biological offspring. By devoting yourself to the nurture or mentoring of another person – which could be another person's child, a younger person from work, school or university – you will grow at the same time.

Lucky People Raise Their Own Level of Stress

Confronting difficulties head on is one way of strengthening luck, and many successful people who achieved great things have experienced hardship in their past.

Thomas Edison, known as the king of inventors, was told by his school headmaster that his brain was addled and made to leave. He was twice let go from jobs for being 'too unproductive'. Albert Einstein, the man who developed the theory of relativity, was not able to talk at age four or speak fluently until he reached high school. He also left high school early and failed entrance examinations to polytechnic school. So many founders of famous corporations have stories of some kind of past hardship that it could be argued they flourish because of it, or that adversity is their springboard.

When the human brain is taxed by a certain level of stress, it tends to make synapses, which are the connecting parts between neurons. When the human body is in a safe and secure state it tries to keep that state constant. But if something happens to threaten that state of security, such as invasion by a virus, our immune cells become activated to fight it. Similarly, brain cells are more active when there is a certain level of stress than in a state of peace and quiet.

The Yerkes–Dodson law confirms this: in an experiment using rats, psychologists Robert Yerkes and John Dodson made the discovery that learning outcomes peak when stress is applied in moderation, but fall with too little or too much stress. The rats were trained to distinguish between black and white, by applying an electric shock whenever they made a mistake. The percentage of correct responses peaked with moderate levels of electric shock and dropped when it was weak or too strong. The results showed a bell-shaped curve in the relationship between stress levels that affect learning performance.

Humans are also more capable of performing under moderate stress than in a safe, uneventful state. For example, it is much easier to focus if a task must be finished by nine o'clock the next day than with an open-ended deadline. If a task is too big, the pressure of responsibility can be overwhelming, but if we are tasked with a more moderate job, all of a sudden a feeling of motivation will kick in.

Yet what counts as moderate stress will vary from person to person. It is important to know your own limits when it comes to what level of stress is appropriate for you. Forcing yourself to perform under circumstances where you feel excessive pressure will not produce good results, and trying too hard in impossible circumstances risks bringing about emotional disturbances such as depression. You must learn to gauge your limits, what is right for you, and what you can afford to take on with a bit of extra effort.

Nevertheless, it is possible to gradually raise your level of tolerance for stress. If you concentrate on studying hard for two hours today, make it two hours

"It is important to know your own limits when it comes to what level of stress is appropriate for you."

and five minutes tomorrow, and then two hours and ten minutes the day after that. If you feel that two hours and ten minutes is your limit on the third day, then stay with two hours and ten minutes on the fourth day. Once you have done two hours and ten minutes comfortably for a few days in a row, challenge yourself to two hours and fifteen minutes. It takes time, but with perseverance it is possible to raise the amount of stress you can tolerate.

Once you have a grasp of your personal stress level – at work, study or other areas of your life – try putting yourself in situations that force you to confront difficult tasks head on. Demanding situations activate the brain cells, raising the likelihood of unexpected outcomes. This, too, is conducive to enhancing your prospects for good luck.

Lucky People Dare to Take Risks

Life can be seen as one long series of choices, and the course of a person's life can change significantly according to the choices they make. Sometimes, luck plays a part in changing it. How should we choose, then? What should we do when we don't know which choice to make? Deliberately choosing a path that seems more risky can be a good approach because the brain tends to enjoy taking risks, as was proved by an experiment with pigeons.

In this experiment, two cages labelled A and B each had a pigeon in them. Both cages had a feed button that dispensed food whenever the pigeons pecked at it with their beak. Cage A dispensed food every time the button was pecked, but cage B sometimes did not, even when the button was pecked. The pigeon in cage A pecked the button only when it was hungry. The pigeon in cage B pecked the button numerous times, irrespective of whether it was hungry or not, doing so most continuously when food came out only 50 per cent of the time, suggesting it had become addicted to pecking the button.

A similar experiment was conducted with monkeys. In this experiment two tanks of juice, labelled A and B, were put in front of a monkey. Tank A consistently dispensed 150ml of juice whenever the button was pressed. Tank B dispensed either 100ml or 200ml when the button was pressed, but the amount could

Lucky People Are Convinced of Their Own Luck

not be selected by the monkey. Under these conditions, the monkey tended to push the button on tank B continuously. Tank B sometimes dispensed only 100ml, but sometimes it dispensed 200ml – more than tank A – so there was risk involved, but also reward if the monkey was lucky. The experiment showed that monkeys tended to select the option that was the biggest gamble.

Humans are believed to have the same tendency. Say there are two members of the opposite sex – call them A and B – who you fancy equally. If you ask A out on a date for dinner or drinks, A accepts 100 per cent of the time, and every time is fun. In contrast, B only accepts 50 per cent of your invitations, but on the occasions when B does accept, you have a really fun time. In this scenario, most people end up preferring B, which perhaps makes sense to you. Someone who is slightly indifferent to you will engage your interest more. You will not be able to stop wondering why your advances are sometimes rejected, or if they have somebody else. You know that next time may also end in rejection, but you are prepared to try again.

Just like the pigeons and monkeys, humans prefer

a situation of slight risk over the 100 per cent safe option. This is because the human brain prefers a situation with a certain amount of risk over one that has no stimulation at all. In psychological terms, it is the application of reinforced learning: something with slight risk activates the brain's reward system.

Next time you are unsure which choice to make, consider taking the slightly riskier option – the path that is a little more adventurous than the safe, reassuring one. Your brain will be happy, you will be more engaged, and the chances of achieving a good result will go up.

Chapter Three

Lucky People Try to Live in Harmony with Others

Lucky People Are Considerate of Others

What kind of person do I want to be? I want to be the kind who checks to see if there are elderly people or pregnant women in the vicinity before taking a seat on a crowded train. Who carefully tilts an umbrella on a rainy street so as not to bump into or shake water onto someone coming the other way. Or who considers the possibility that I overlooked something when a problem arises at work, rather than declaring I did everything possible. That is the kind of person I want to be.

My aim is to not simply be concerned with my own welfare, but to care about other people's as well. People who do this don't look to draw attention to what they do or make a display of it, but rather try to integrate it seamlessly into the small acts of daily life. Anyone who can do this, it could be argued, can be called a lucky person. This is the lesson that the story of Neanderthal man teaches us.

The Neanderthals are regarded as one subspecies

"My aim is to not simply be concerned with my own welfare, but to care about other people's as well."

of modern-day humans, i.e. *Homo sapiens*, who lived mainly in Europe and the Middle East approximately 200,000 to 30,000 years ago. The reason they became extinct is still a mystery, but one theory is that they were annihilated by the Cro-Magnons, another branch of contemporary humans.

Neanderthals had a larger brain than modern man, with the average volume for a male Neanderthal being 1,500 cubic centimetres, compared to 1,400 in male *Homo sapiens*. Until recently it was believed that aggression was a trait of the smaller-brained *Homo sapiens*, and the most likely reason they survived while the Neanderthals did not. Today, we know that Neanderthals' brains were bigger overall, but the section known as the frontal lobe was larger in *Homo sapiens'* brains.

The frontal lobe is responsible for linguistic activity, movement and mental activity, among other things, but the section of it known as the prefrontal cortex is particularly important for thought and creativity. This is what gives us the ability to project into the future and plan accordingly, concepts of altruism and sociability, and other such defining human thought traits. The current view is that the larger frontal lobe enabled

Lucky People

Homo sapiens to survive because of a more advanced sociability than Neanderthals.

It is easier for a single male to survive than it is for a whole community. If a single male is strong enough to escape from enemies such as wolves, and to secure enough food, he will be able to survive. But for his seed to survive, he must protect the women and children because survival as a community is required. For this to happen, a social sense that drives everyone to co-operate and survive is necessary. The Neanderthals did not have a social nature like this and so they lost out in the game of evolution.

The same can be said of companies or individual shops: survival is one form of good luck. One survival lesson we can learn from the difference between the two brains of Neanderthals and *Homo sapiens* is that it is important to care about others rather than only yourself, to be mutually considerate, and to be sociable so that everybody can be steered into co-operating.

Lucky People Try to Live in Harmony with Others

Lucky People Don't Try to Be the Only Winner

We have already seen that compassion and sociability are necessary qualities for survival, but these alone are not enough. Consider corporations that operate on the premise of performing some function useful to society. If a company's sole concern is its social duty and it pays no regard to profit, it will eventually go bankrupt. Similarly, a person who gives all their food away to others and eats nothing themselves will eventually fall sick. In other words, to survive you must first be successful yourself, and then you must continue to be so.

What can you do, then, to keep on winning while continuing to be compassionate and caring towards others? The secret is to not be too successful.

Of course, adapting to your environment is necessary to survive, but excessive adaptation, or over-adaptation, carries with it the risk of extinction. We can express this as 'better is better than best': although the best strategy will result in victory for a time, it is highly likely to be doomed in the long term. Therefore, the best choice is the better path rather than the best one.

One example of this is the African black rhinoceros. Each individual animal has a large, swift body and can be a fierce, aggressive and extremely strong fighter in battle, making it the strongest of species. Yet sudden changes in the environment meant even an indomitable creature like the black rhinoceros rapidly became a critically endangered species. Because each black rhinoceros is a highly capable fighter, there was almost no danger of losing its life in the struggle for existence once it reached maturity. Given these parameters, the best strategy for the species' survival was to give birth just a few times, take good care of any calves and raise them into strong, healthy adults. There was no advantage to having numerous offspring because giving birth multiple times is a major physical strain on the mother and increases her chances of being attacked in the post-partum period when she is weaker and more vulnerable. Calves, too, are most at risk before reaching adulthood; after all the time, labour and effort expended on having babies, if there were too many calves for parents to keep an eye on they would be at much greater risk of attack from lions and hyenas.

In fact, the black rhino's seemingly optimal basic

> *We can express this as 'better is better than best': although the best strategy will result in victory for a time, it is highly likely to be doomed in the long term.*

survival strategy led to a precarious situation known as over-adaptation; once the environment changed, the black rhino became endangered. This change was brought about by the arrival of humans – a catastrophic event of enormous significance for the rhinos. Faced with the arrival of a natural predator, the rhinos would have been able to adapt over time to changed conditions, but human beings did not allow them time to readjust. Instead, the rhinos' environment was destroyed at a speed that exceeded their natural power of adaptation, as if a giant meteor had fallen to Earth. The over-adapted black rhino was unable to withstand such extreme changes to its environment and in no time at all became a critically endangered species. Being perfectly adapted to one environment was no guarantee of being able to endure and thrive in a new one that required a 'better' adaptation and leeway for change. An existence that relied on complete dominance in a certain set of circumstances was over-adaptation to the environment, and that existence suddenly became precarious when conditions changed and the animal was unable to cope.

The same can be said of human society. Corporations

Lucky People Try to Live in Harmony with Others

or countries at the peak of domination in one era will inevitably founder. Win too much and you cannot continue to win. This is why we should choose the path that allows for more than one winner, and does not lead to excessive victory – the path where everybody gets to survive, rather than one where the winners care only about their own survival and nobody else's. If you can find a way to skilfully coexist with those around you, this will secure your continued survival in the long run.

Lucky People Behave Graciously

Always behave graciously, because at certain decisive moments this will bear fruit. This means things like opening and closing the door quietly, handling money with care when paying in a shop, always speaking politely (even to people you know well), and pressing on the car horn gently if you must use it out of necessity. It means always being conscious of conducting yourself with dignity and consideration in all daily life because, in many instances, such behaviour will lead to a favourable outcome. The tit-for-tat strategy in game theory proves this.

Game theory is a mathematical analysis of how parties should act to maximise their own interests and value in situations (i.e. the game) such as price competition and negotiations involving multiple parties (i.e. the decision-makers). The basics of it were developed by mathematician John von Neumann and economist Oskar Morgenstern in the mid-twentieth century. Today, its applications include identifying the key factors when it comes to making optimal choices in policy-making and business.

Say Company A purchases stock of a product supplied by Company B. They engage in price negotiations, and naturally A wants to purchase at the lowest possible price while B wants to get the highest price they can. If there is only one round of negotiations, A goes for the lowest price and B for the highest. But if this is not a one-time transaction, and there is to be any future dealing, that is not the wisest policy. There has to be an optimal price that, based on relations between the two companies, takes into account the situation for each and allows them both to pursue profit. This can be derived mathematically in game theory.

The tit-for-tat strategy is a method in game theory

Lucky People Try to Live in Harmony with Others

that maximises mutual benefits. The basic tactic is to be co-operative with the opponent, retaliate when they betray you, but immediately revert to being co-operative when they do.

Say two people are competing for points in a game of 'rock paper scissors', but in this case there are only two choices: rock or paper. Points are awarded for each potential outcome, as shown in brackets below.

Pattern 1:	rock (2)	vs.	rock (2)
Pattern 2:	rock (0)	vs.	paper (3)
Pattern 3:	paper (3)	vs.	rock (0)
Pattern 4:	paper (1)	vs.	paper (1)

If the aim is simply to win outright, the best approach is to continually play paper. But if the aim is for each side to score as many points as possible, the tit-for-tat method can work. In a strategy of joint co-operation like this, the first play would be rock. You continue to play rock for as long as your opponent does, but if the opponent plays paper, so do you – and you continue to do so. If your opponent switches back to rock, so do you. This method results in each party scoring the maximum possible points. In this approach you don't try to knock your opponent out from the start, but stay one step behind. Don't fight dirty, but graciously and with a sense of civility. Ultimately it leads to gains for both parties.

There is plenty of scope to apply this method of sparring in daily life: asking a work colleague to do something for you; putting in a request to your boss for annual leave; asking a spouse to share in the housework; or speaking to the neighbours about toning down the noise. In any situation, rather than trying to get one over the other party with a victory that benefits only you, it is better to conduct yourself in a civil and well-behaved manner with the aim of achieving mutual benefit for all. If the person next door suddenly storms over, complaining about noise, your most likely reaction is to also become angry without really understanding the problem, but if they approach you and speak in a quiet and civilised manner, you are more inclined to hear them out. Polite, civilised behaviour is always more likely to move someone than rudeness.

Lucky People Try to Live in Harmony with Others

Lucky People Wish for Their Rivals to Prosper

Do you have friends who are also rivals? If so, can you say – hand on heart – that you hope for their success? If someone is going for the same promotion, a regular spot in the same sports team, or has feelings for the same person as you, and they are unmistakably a rival, it may be difficult to truly hope that person does well. Perhaps deep down you really want them to fail. If so, you need to dispense with that sentiment and sincerely wish them well instead, because this is what will lead to your own success.

The human brain has a fundamental desire to live in harmony. Humans have been coexisting with other creatures ever since their appearance on the planet 250,000 years ago, but for the last few hundred years the human ego has become such a threat to the environment that many plants and animals have been driven to extinction. For most of mankind's long history, we have shared the environment with other animals and plants in a successful coexistence; indeed, our coexistence with other plants and animals has enabled human survival.

"Do you have friends who are also rivals? If so, can you say – hand on heart – that you hope for their success?"

American neuroscientist Paul MacLean proposed the triune theory, the idea that the human brain is three brains in one and evolved along with changes in behavioural patterns. He divided the brain into three, as follows:

- The reptilian brain, composed of the brain stem, a section of the thalamus, and striatum. It is responsible for such basic life-sustaining functions as breathing, heart rate, body-temperature regulation, reflexes and sensory information processing.
- The paleomammalian (old mammal) brain, composed of structures in the limbic system such as amygdala, hypothalamus and hippocampus. It is responsible for memory and learning, fear, uncertainty, pleasure, and the flight-from-danger reaction.
- The neomammalian (new mammal) brain, a section of the neocortex. It enables thought, language, adaptability and planning.

MacLean put forward the hypothesis that the human brain evolved sequentially in the order of reptilian brain, paleomammalian brain, and then neomammalian brain. The oldest part of the brain (the reptilian brain) enabled survival, the paleomammalian brain advanced evolution one step forward from survival of the individual to preservation of the species, and then the neomammalian brain – the part regarded as having the most distinctively human traits – is geared towards coexistence and facilitating smooth social relations. All told, it evolved along a path that started from self-survival, towards coexistence with others.

The brain performs better when the goal is coexistence rather than fighting and prevailing over others, which is why we should wish for our rivals to grow and develop. Rivalry and competition – be it in sports, work or life – will stimulate you into delivering your best performance. If someone is your rival in a sports competition, hope that they deliver the best possible performance. If someone is aiming to join the same company or enter the same university as you, think of them as your partner in a joint struggle, and hope for you both to succeed. If you are both rivals for the affections of the same person, you may find it difficult to hope the other person will succeed, but you

" The brain performs better when the goal is coexistence rather than fighting and prevailing over others, which is why we should wish for our rivals to grow and develop."

could look at it from another angle, and hope that all three of you end up going in the direction that's best for each of you. Wishing for the happiness of the three of you, rather than simply for yourself, enables your brain to perform more effectively.

Lucky People Are Altruistic

To what extent are you prepared to live your life for others? To what extent are you able to be altruistic enough to put aside your own interests temporarily in order to act in other people's? This behaviour seems to have a big influence on luck, because when people behave altruistically, many good things occur in the brain.

One such good thing can be that the brain's reward system is stimulated, since doing things for other people can result in receiving praise and approval, and to the human brain this is equivalent to the joy of receiving cash.

This was demonstrated by Professor Norihiro Sadato's research group at the National Institute for Physiological Sciences in Okazaki, Aichi prefecture. The team used magnetic resonance imaging (MRI) to

Lucky People Try to Live in Harmony with Others

observe changes to blood in the brain, examining the respective effects on the brain of receiving a cash prize and of being praised. A test group of nineteen male and female subjects with an average age of twenty-one received prize money in a card game, and were shown words of praise on a small monitor. Both situations activated a part of the striatum, the part of the reward system involved with producing pleasure, indicating that the brain perceives praise as a reward.

Countless experiments and research have also made it clear that stimulation of the reward system activates natural killer cells, with beneficial effects to the body. Yet there is no guarantee that altruistic behaviour will always be rewarded with praise and approval, and in many instances nobody sees what we do for others. Even if nobody else is a witness, you still see yourself, and your brain can still experience pleasure from self-praise. This happens when the area of the brain called the medial prefrontal cortex is activated. This part, which is involved with assessment of our own actions, can experience great pleasure from self-praise.

Other people expressing happiness about your altruistic conduct also activates the reward system in our brain. When people with experience of volunteering are asked 'When was the best moment?', common responses are 'When the other person was happy,' and 'Being thanked.' Feeling other people's joy as your own can be attributed to the activation of mirror neurons, as we saw earlier. When you engage in altruistic behaviour and receive a positive evaluation as a result – and when the recipient of your behaviour is pleased – the brain experiences multiple levels of joy all at once.

Professor Satoshi Fujii of Kyoto University conducted a psychological study that classified people based on what they focused on deep in their hearts. He wrote that people who show concern for others have good fortune, and concluded that the broader the range of their concern, the luckier they were. The range of concern was defined by positioning the current self as the point of origin, with human relations and time as axes. Human relations were ranked according to their social and psychological distance: family and romantic partners were closest, with distance gradually increasing from friends, to work colleagues or school classmates, to acquaintances, and then finally strangers. The time axis showed the extent of a person's

Lucky People Try to Live in Harmony with Others

thoughts about the future. People do not think only about today; their thoughts also project into the future, such as two or three days from now, or next year. They think about the future of their parents, their children, and – in the case of some people – about the future of society as a whole.

Fujii focused on the degree to which a person's luck was apparently determined by the breadth of their ability to be concerned about others, and for how far ahead. Those who think only about themselves, with no interest in anything other than immediate losses and gains, have a narrow range of concern. In contrast, those who are also able to think about the future of family, friends, strangers and the whole of society have a much broader range of concern. While those with narrow ranges of concern were able to produce results, these were limited when compared to those with a broader range of concerns, because the former group's fixation on immediate concerns prevented them from building co-operative relationships. As a result, their lives, on the whole, had significant losses that prevented them from achieving a sense of happiness. Conversely, altruistically oriented people with a broader range of concern were able to create an enduring solid network due to their ability to build and maintain the kind of personal relations that are conducive to good luck.

When it comes to improving luck, this teaches us that you should put yourself in the shoes of family and friends, and not think solely of yourself. Don't think only of family and friends, though, but also be considerate of workmates, juniors and bosses. Then don't think only of your workmates, but let your thoughts extend to people in the neighbourhood and staff in the shops you frequent. Don't think only of people in the neighbourhood; think about people living in the same town as you whose faces and names you don't know. Finally, think of people living around the world, not just in your own town and country, and be mindful of their future too.

Lucky People Sincerely Compliment Others

Lucky people are skilful at complimenting others, doing it readily and sincerely. If they think someone is amazing or lovely, they will tell that person so immediately. If a friend is wearing something nice,

Lucky People Try to Live in Harmony with Others

they will say on the spot, 'I like the outfit you're wearing today.' If they are impressed with someone's attitude or point of view, they will tell them, 'I really admire your attitude.' People who can praise others sincerely and appropriately will be liked in turn.

You have probably heard of Wallis Simpson (1896–1986), who leapt to prominence as the American woman who fell in love with King Edward VIII and cost him the crown. Wallis and Edward wanted to marry but her history of divorce, and the fact that she was still married when their affair began, meant the British royal family, prime minister and many English citizens opposed it. Forced into choosing between the throne or marriage with Wallis, Edward decided to abdicate. At the time it was the biggest scandal of the twentieth century and was reported as headline news in newspapers around the world.

What was it about Wallis that made Edward willing to give up the crown and fulfil his desire to spend the rest of his life with her? One theory is that she was uncommonly skilled at complimenting people. I wonder if perhaps Wallis's praise of Edward made him feel understood as a human being for the first time in his life. Naturally, everyone around Edward, including the royal family, treated him as heir to the throne or as king after his ascension. But before being a king he was also a man, and I think Wallis saw this clearly, loving him not for his crown or position but for the person himself. The words of praise that sprang from this won his heart.

Wallis Simpson may be an extreme example, but it makes a point: we do not think badly of people who praise or compliment us. If anything, we are favourably disposed towards them because it is human nature to like the social reward of being complimented or valued by someone.

This was proved by an experiment called 'The Dictator Game'. The game is played in pairs, with one person designated as the dictator. The dictator is given a certain sum of money and told to split it with the other person. The dictator has complete licence to divide it as they like. The other person has no say or right in the decision and can make no changes. If you were the dictator, how would you divide it? Experiments show most people choose to split it evenly, or close to even. Almost no one acts solely in their own self-interest by giving themselves the lion's share. Most people choose the course that would result in their being thought of as good or virtuous rather than stingy, choosing the social reward over the financial reward.

When someone sincerely praises someone else, it gives them a social reward that in turn naturally makes them attractive to the person they praised. That is why we should heap praise on others. If you think someone is great, don't hesitate to tell them. There is nothing to be gained from keeping such thoughts to yourself; it is important to speak them out loud, directly to the other person.

Lucky People Are Tolerant of Faults and Praise Strengths

While praising others may be a good thing, it must be done with care, because random, inappropriate compliments can have the opposite effect, and so there are several things to be careful of.

The first thing is to offer praise that is true. Compliments only make people happy when they are convincing to the person themselves. Praising someone for being delicate when they actually think of themselves as rough and slapdash will come across as being off the mark, making them feel misjudged. The brain's reward system reacts to compliments and makes you feel good, but this doesn't happen when words of praise ring false.

The second thing is to not give praise lightly or superficially. On hearing I am a graduate of Tokyo University, some people immediately say, 'Oh, you must be smart.' But being told this does not make me happy. If anything, it makes me uneasy because I wonder if that person is judging me through the filter of my education rather than as a person.

The third thing is to be tolerant of faults and praise, as the following child psychology experiment highlights. A group of primary schoolchildren were divided into two subgroups, A and B, with a teacher assigned to each. Each subgroup included a girl who was very good at schoolwork and a boy who was extremely poor at it. Group A's teacher thoroughly praised Girl C, who was good at schoolwork – giving comments such as 'What a good girl' and 'That's wonderful' – but scolded Boy D in the same group, who was extremely poor at schoolwork,

Lucky People Try to Live in Harmony with Others

with comments like 'Why can't you do such an easy problem,' and 'Useless child.' Group B's teacher used similar language to group A's teacher when thoroughly praising Girl E, who was good at schoolwork, but with Boy F, who was not so good at schoolwork, she remarked on his strengths with comments such as 'You might not be able to do maths well but you know a lot about insects' and 'You're good at drawing.'

Girls C and E were both praised similarly but Girl E was the happier. Though glad of the praise, Girl C was also nervous about being scolded if her schoolwork deteriorated or the teacher found something else to pick fault with. Girl E, meanwhile, could sense that even if her schoolwork dipped, the teacher would still recognise other strengths, and that she would not be pressured on her weaknesses.

All human beings have strengths and weaknesses, but the degree to which we feel happy at receiving compliments on our strengths is moderated by how our weaknesses are evaluated. Say your partner compliments your intelligence but also notes that you tend to be careless about punctuality. Would it make you happier to be told that 'You are really intelligent, but you must do something about your terrible unpunctuality,' or that 'I'd be worn out if you were punctual as well as intelligent, so never mind, it's fine'? The latter, of course.

It is easy to criticise others' faults; becoming tolerant of them requires a little more effort, though. But it is important to be able to do this if you are to be liked and live in harmony with others.

Lucky People Are Adept at Managing Anxiety

Praising others may sound simple enough, but a certain degree of mental leeway is necessary to be able to compliment others both sincerely and accurately. If your mind is completely focused on yourself, you won't view others with sufficient neutrality. It is also harder to notice their good points.

Anxiety tends to preoccupy people's minds. Will I pass the exams? Will things go OK at work? Is my partner cheating on me? Do I have enough money? Can I stay healthy my whole life? Our lives are filled with any number of anxieties about all kinds of things.

"All human beings have strengths and weaknesses, but the degree to which we feel happy at receiving compliments on our strengths is moderated by how our weaknesses are evaluated."

When we are overanxious, not only is it impossible to offer anyone else sincere praise, but we can tend to take our dissatisfaction out on people who haven't noticed our anxiety or on partners who are unable to help. So the first step is to deal with any anxiety. If you are feeling anxious, recognise that your mind is overwhelmed and try the following coping strategies.

Cultivate daily habits that increase serotonin production

The secret to increasing serotonin is to lead a regular lifestyle that involves going to bed early and rising early, moderate amounts of exercise, and relaxing in the bath. See the section Lucky People Are Early to Bed and Early to Rise for more detail (p. 69).

Be clear when your anxiety is due to menstruation

Serotonin production is believed to decrease in women prior to menstruation, so recognising this as a likely cause of anxiety at such a time is one way to handle it. Rather than dwelling on the fact of being anxious and worrying about things, remind yourself that it is simply a physiological phenomenon due to a decrease

Lucky People Try to Live in Harmony with Others

in serotonin, just as feeling hungry or menstrual pain is. Use this knowledge as a tool to gain more control at a trying time and to prevent yourself falling into a vicious cycle of anxiety building on anxiety.

Try changing the way you perceive your anxiety

Most people would prefer to be free of anxiety, but anxiety can also be thought of as an essential life function. Being anxious is one aspect of being able to prepare, plan and make effort. Thoughts of what might happen if we get ill motivate us to lead healthier lives. The fear of what would happen if we lost our job drives us to work harder to avoid being laid off. And worry about what might happen if our partner has an affair prompts us to make a nest egg just in case.

Suppressing the secretion of serotonin may be the brain's way of not allowing us to become too laid back. Viewed in this way, anxiety is not all bad.

Put anxiety out of your mind

Some kinds of anxiety are vague and hard to identify, so trying to view yourself objectively can help. If you are anxious, be aware that this is what you are feeling, then visualise it as something physical that can be separated from your body. Say to yourself, 'I know I'm experiencing anxiety right now, and there's so much I should think about, but for now I'm going to put this anxiety out of my mind and sleep tonight – I will worry about things later.' In many cases, when you come back the next morning after a good night's sleep, the anxiety will be gone.

Lucky People Thank Those They Help

As we have already seen, lucky people do not ride roughshod over others or aim to be the sole winners; rather they try to live in harmony with other people. For luck to be on your side, therefore, it is important to be considerate and understanding of others, to be helpful and behave altruistically. An attitude of gratitude is also required when helping others. Perhaps you think it is the person being helped who should be thankful; in fact, the person offering the help is the one who should feel grateful.

Actions that involve outsmarting someone so that you alone can benefit – such as riding roughshod

"If you are anxious, be aware that this is what you are feeling, then visualise it as something physical that can be separated from your body."

over work colleagues so that only you can achieve promotion, or taking a seat in the train while there is an elderly passenger standing who you pretend not to see – can make you feel pained at the recognition you 'did something bad'. Conversely, doing something for the benefit of friends with their welfare in mind, or giving up your seat to an elderly person, will make you feel good because of the self-recognition that you 'did something good'.

As we have already seen, your brain's medial prefrontal cortex passes judgement on your actions. When it decides you have done something good, the brain's reward system kicks in, creating a good mood or a feeling of satisfaction with your own conduct. When you help somebody, it is judged as 'good' and your mood is lifted. When the recipient of your help shows their appreciation, the social reward you gain is significant. Doing things for other people can initially seem like self-sacrifice because of the time, effort and occasionally expense involved, but the truth is that you lift your own spirits through helping someone else and sometimes receiving the social reward.

Something else to keep in mind when helping others

Lucky People Try to Live in Harmony with Others

is the reciprocity principle. Because human beings are by nature reciprocal, and repay each other for rewards received, they feel compelled to repay when they are a beneficiary. Think of food tastings in the supermarket: if you accept a sample and eat it, you might feel bad if you then leave without buying a packet of the food, even if you didn't like it. If the whole family is with you and everyone has a taste, you will end up buying the product even though you might not want to. Or say a friend brings you back a souvenir from their holiday; when you go on your own holiday, you feel bad if you don't buy something for them as well. Even knowing that the other person did not give you a souvenir with the expectation of receiving one in return, it doesn't feel right unless you repay them in some way.

When we are on the receiving end of help, we feel as if we have incurred a debt. We are extremely uncomfortable remaining in this state because subconsciously we know there is a social penalty for people who do not return favours – they are disliked. This means the act of helping somebody is equivalent to putting an obligation on them. The recipient may well be truly grateful, but at the same time they also feel bad, or obliged to return the favour. Helping people is noble, but we must remember the burden it puts on the recipient. That is why it is important to have a spirit of humility and be grateful for 'being allowed to help' the other person.

Also remember to accept thanks from the other person graciously. Allow them to repay their gratitude, or their feeling of indebtedness to you will become an uncomfortable burden and they may end up feeling that any relationship with you is too onerous. By accepting their thanks, you can lighten the burden on them.

Chapter Four

Lucky People Set Their Own Standards for Happiness

Lucky People Have Concrete Aims

Although luck has a highly unscientific image, many scientists do still want to be lucky. The word 'serendipity' itself was at one time very popular in Japan, and is defined as 'making happy and unexpected discoveries by accident' or 'attracting good fortune'. We can think of it as the ability to grasp accidental good luck.

There are many examples of serendipitous major discoveries in the world of science. The co-recipient of the 2000 Nobel Prize in Chemistry, Hideki Shirakawa, discovered a plastic that can conduct electricity (formally 'the discovery and development of conductive polymers') with an accidental oversight in an experiment that led to a major innovation. Dr Shirakawa was an assistant research associate in 1967 at the Tokyo Institute of Technology when he provided a visiting research student with the protocol for an experiment to synthesise polyacetylene, a kind of plastic. The experiment failed, producing a substance that was more like a black rag than the black powder that was expected. This result intrigued Shirakawa, who was inspired to conduct a series of further experiments to determine the cause of the failure. In the course of these, he found that changing the concentration of catalyst resulted in the formation of a metallic film, a discovery that eventually led to the Nobel prize-winning research.

Similarly, a failed experiment also led to a major discovery for Koichi Tanaka of the Shimadzu Corporation, co-winner of the Nobel Prize in Chemistry in 2002 for the development of soft laser desorption ionisation methods for macromolecules (a technique facilitating the weight analysis of biomolecules). Tanaka made an error when he was working on an experiment, and mistakenly mixed ultra-fine metal powder into a solution he was using. Though he immediately realised his error, he decided to continue with the experiment because it would be wasteful to discard the solution, and this led to new breakthroughs.

These two cases are just a tiny fraction of examples of serendipity in the world of science. There are many other scientists – and indeed countless people in all

Lucky People Set Their Own Standards for Happiness

industries and fields – whose benefiting from random good fortune has powerfully demonstrated the results of serendipity.

People who benefit from serendipitous occurrences are often called lucky, but arguably they also share common traits that are key to enhancing their luck. If there is a god of luck, these people have done the work that prepares them to catch any arrows of good fortune shot off by this god. The most important factor in being prepared is to have a clear aim, and to never forget it; these people have an unwavering awareness of what they want to do and achieve. Hideki Shirakawa had wanted to study macromolecules and create a new plastic ever since he was in middle school. This was only one of many things he wanted to do, but if he had not had the idea at all he never would have had the serendipitous fortune that he did. In Koichi Tanaka's case, the research group he belonged to at work had a major goal: the ionisation of a sample with a molecular weight of 10,000.

Having a set goal is what makes the concrete efforts needed to achieve it possible. Insight about what is required arises from the process of thinking about how it can be done, which in turn stimulates creativity and invention. Curiosity and an unwillingness to give up are also essential. In short, a lot of groundwork preparation is required, but it all starts from having a concrete aim – nothing can begin without that. The god of fortune is unlikely to shoot off any arrows where there is no target to begin with.

Lucky People Set Their Own Standards for Happiness

Having your own standards for happiness is another vital aspect of having goals. You must be able to decide your goals in accordance with your own criteria.

First, let's consider the kinds of situations in which phrases such as 'good luck' and 'bad luck' are used. Say somebody hits the jackpot in the lottery: according to just the bare facts – i.e. they won a large amount of money – this person can be called lucky. But the reality may not be quite so straightforward: the winner might have an enormous debt that exceeds the prize money, or perhaps they already possess great wealth, or maybe the win ends up turning their life upside down and

Lucky People Set Their Own Standards for Happiness

destroying relations with relatives. Alternatively, other people would be able to use a big windfall effectively and become happier as a result. In other words, good luck is not something that can be objectively defined. Ultimately it is up to the individual to decide if the circumstances they find themselves in constitute good luck or bad.

So how do people come to feel they are unlucky? A major reason, I believe, is not having a goal that aligns with their own criteria for happiness. With no clear idea of what their own values are, there is nothing to use as a basis for decisions about what constitutes happiness for them and what they want. People who are not clear on their own values are easily influenced by others' values and general opinion.

There is a story about a couple who won a huge jackpot worth millions. They were both working in a factory, which they ended up buying with their winnings. Perhaps they were hoping for a dazzlingly successful transition from employee to employer. Several years on, however, burdened with debt in excess of what they had won, they went bankrupt. Why did they buy the factory? Were they swayed perhaps by the

" People who are not clear on their own values are easily influenced by others' values and general opinion."

Lucky People Set Their Own Standards for Happiness

general view that being a boss is better than being an employee? Perhaps someone said, 'You should buy the factory' and that persuaded them. I don't know what they really thought, but if this couple had had goals based on their own standards of happiness, they might not have chosen to buy the factory.

Similar arguments can be made about appearance: if a woman is very good-looking, other people feel they can make ill-thought-out and irresponsible comments such as 'you should become a model'. If that woman finds the work of being a model worthwhile, then following the path to become one could lead to happiness for her. But if she becomes a model merely because of what other people say, at some point she will be beset by doubts and wonder if she chose the right profession.

If you do not have goals or aims that measure up against your own standards of happiness, the chances and opportunities that come your way may be wasted. If someone is under the influence of others' opinions, then their money, academic background, titles and good looks are tools that can be used mistakenly, paving the way for unhappy or unfortunate outcomes.

When Koichi Tanaka received the Nobel Prize, he

was forty-three years old and in a low-level managerial position. A lot of people might consider anyone over the age of forty and still at that level to have given up ambitions of career progression. Tanaka, however, did not choose to be on the promotion track, because he preferred to work with his hands on the floor. He liked doing experiments, assembling equipment himself and meeting directly with clients to explain the products. In his view, this was more valuable to him than anything else. Without this strong sense of his own values, he would not have been working in the laboratory and done the work that led to a Nobel Prize. So ask yourself: what dream do you want to achieve? What are the goals or aims that you live for? How do these measure up against your own standards for happiness? If you are going to catch the arrows of good fortune, you must start by affirming these.

Lucky People Don't Give Up the Game

One way of looking at our lives is to see them as a series of games, such as exams, job-hunting, finding a partner, or family life. If you stop working, for example, the

Lucky People Set Their Own Standards for Happiness

game called 'work' comes to an end. While we are always participating in several games at once, lucky people will never withdraw by choice from the game they consider to be the crucial one. The crucial game is the one that aligns with your goals as measured against your standards for happiness.

J. K. Rowling is now a world-famous author of the Harry Potter series, but when she wrote the first book, *Harry Potter and the Philosopher's Stone*, she was still an unknown. From a very young age she liked to write, but her circumstances were never ideal for concentrating on writing. A troubled marriage ended in divorce and she became a single mother, living in hardship and afflicted with depression. Despite these difficulties, she did not give up on writing novels, and wrote the first Harry Potter book while in recovery from depression and receiving welfare assistance. Her manuscript was initially rejected by twelve publishers before being accepted and going on to become an international bestseller and the start of a series. J. K. Rowling remarried and now ranks among the wealthiest people in Britain. Some might argue that she had talent to begin with, and that is why she could succeed. Yet, no matter how much talent she had, if she had dropped out of the game of becoming an author, her dream would not have been realised.

Staying in the game is vital. It's a very simple thing, but no lucky person will give up the game easily. It is understandable to want to give up when the path to your dreams consists of one failure after another, but the secret to not doing so is to think of life as being like the random walk model.

As we saw on page 8, when you throw a coin, each side has a one-in-two chance of turning up. Imagine this plotted on a graph. Throw a coin 10,000 times, and each time it comes up heads, plot a point in the plus direction; each time tails comes up, plot a point in the minus direction. If you join up the points, what shape does the path take? Most people tend to picture it as weaving to and fro in a narrow range centred around zero, but since it is possible for the points to fall in a wide range from minus 10,000 to plus 10,000, there is only a very slight probability that zero will be the central point. Try actually throwing a coin and you will see that in many cases it settles into a shape of plus 200–300 times or minus 200–300 times.

Lucky People Set Their Own Standards for Happiness

Think of the path to your goals as being like this: the minus direction is when there are setbacks, and the plus direction is when progress and good things happen. Just as with tossing a coin, there are many times when you will experience either one negative thing after another, or a streak of one positive thing after another. Over the long term, however, there will always be negatives and positives, and the results will fall roughly half on the positive side and roughly half on the negative.

Unlucky people do not take the long-term view and so they withdraw from the game when they hit a run of negative events. Lucky people will not drop out of the game so easily, even after a series of negative events. Instead, when they continue to lose, they endeavour to minimise the loss while preparing for the next opportunity. In the long term, good and bad occurs in almost equal proportion for us all, but unlucky people drop out of the game midway, while lucky people do not give up until the last. The result is that lucky people have even more luck, while unlucky people's fortunes get worse. Striking it lucky is not the result of inherent good luck, but rather simply the difference between staying in the game or not.

Be prepared for the path to achieving your dreams and goals to be like the random walk model. There may be times when it seems as if one bad thing after another is happening, but bear in mind that there will certainly come a time when things swing the other way. In the meantime, think of what you can do now to prepare for that time when it comes. Or, if you are in the middle of a good streak now, continue to push ahead and do not let your attention waver. Be persistent; stay in the game. This is the secret to ultimate victory.

Lucky People Know That the Brain Gets Bored

Staying in the game is important but, as with any game, there are enemies who will bring you down. The greatest of these is boredom.

The human brain will naturally become quickly used to a particular stimulation and grow bored. Even if common sayings such as 'persistence pays off' and 'practice makes perfect' are true, it does not alter the fact that it can still be difficult to continue because the brain gets bored. But making skilful use of the

"There may be times when it seems as if one bad thing after another is happening, but bear in mind that there will certainly come a time when things swing the other way."

brain's reward system and continually supplying it with new stimulation can prevent this.

Let's think about this in relation to language learning. Perhaps you have tried to study a foreign language as an adult and failed to get very far. Continuity is crucial when learning another language, but it's also the hardest of things to do. I began studying French at the age of thirty-two. My second foreign language at university was German, so with French I was truly starting from scratch. When it looked as if the opportunity to work at the Saclay Nuclear Research Centre was really going to happen, I was under pressure to learn French. I had about a year until beginning work in France, during which time I managed to acquire enough language to get by in everyday life.

I began by listing various activities that an ability to speak French would allow me to do: swan into a cafe by myself and order a drink and cake of my choice without fear, or discuss interesting research with my colleagues. And wouldn't it be cool if I were able to give a speech in French like 1994 Nobel Prize winner Kenzaburō Ōe! I decided I was absolutely going to show people I could do this! New language learners

Lucky People Set Their Own Standards for Happiness

often have the vague goal of 'being able to speak'. But, at heart, language is purely an instrument for communication, and as such it is vital to think in concrete terms about what you want to do with this instrument, and the kinds of situations you want to be in. Make these your goal and continue to keep in mind an image of yourself achieving them.

Next, I thought about what the most pressing thing was for me to make my goal a reality, and began by studying pronunciation. Once I had a grasp of pronunciation, all the sounds that had previously sounded like a soufflé of noise to me suddenly took on meaning. This was incredibly exciting. Then I began on grammar and set myself the goal of mastering one thin grammar book. (If I'd chosen a thick one, I probably would not have finished it, but completing one book of grammar – however thin – produced a feeling of achievement: *'I did it!*) With an understanding of the basics under my belt, I decided I'd like to correspond with a French person and become fluent enough to be able to convey my thoughts and ideas in written French. I looked about for a cyberfriend and began exchanging emails, which was a great experience in learning living French.

Though I was not conscious of it at the time, my method of study dovetailed neatly with the brain's needs, as step by step I gave it fresh stimulation through studying pronunciation, grammar, and then writing emails. Approaching the language from a different angle each time meant my brain never became bored. Moreover, the whole process of being able to understand the meaning of words once I had a grasp of pronunciation, and to speak a little once I could handle grammar, was incredibly absorbing. My brain's reward system was stimulated into producing dopamine, the origin of motivation, which spurred me on to do more.

This method of studying French made use of the brain's inherent nature: retaining a firm memory of actions that bring pleasure, and repeating that action to experience the same pleasure. This same principle and method can be effectively applied to help you stay in the game to achieve your dreams and goals. Make your brain happy by giving it fresh stimulus. Always make the effort to think about something new – such as tweaks for improvement, or different approaches to the task – and try to enjoy yourself. This will prevent

"Make your brain happy by giving it fresh stimulus. Always make the effort to think about something new – such as tweaks for improvement, or different approaches to the task."

the brain from becoming bored, and will bring you closer to your dreams and goals.

Lucky People Accept Setbacks

Something else that lucky people have in common is their ability to accept setbacks. No matter how lucky a person may be, everybody experiences sadness, failure, setbacks, difficult partings and other hardships at some time in their life. The difference between lucky people and unlucky people lies in how they cope with these.

Take Masatoshi Koshiba, joint winner of the 2002 Nobel Prize in Physics. A pioneer in detecting cosmic neutrinos who helped found the new field of neutrino astronomy, he is also regarded as a very lucky man. Neutrinos are a cosmic elementary particle believed to hold the key to understanding the mysteries of the universe. They were formed during a supernova explosion in the Large Magellanic Cloud 160,000 years ago, travelling an enormous distance and now pouring down continually in large amounts onto Earth, where they pass through our bodies, but they are extremely difficult to detect. Koshiba helped design a giant

Lucky People Set Their Own Standards for Happiness

neutron detector for what is known as the Kamiokande experiment (designed to search for decaying protons), and in February 1987 successfully detected neutrinos for the first time. They were detected by the Kamiokande due to the coincidence of several pieces of good luck: Koshiba was still working, but due to retire in one month; he had recently begun operating the Kamiokande detector, and the neutrinos flew into it at just the right time, not when magnetic tape used to record observations was being replaced.

Koshiba's successful detection of neutrinos cannot solely be attributed to luck, but a groundwork built on long years of meticulous preparation, steady effort, fresh ideas and being proactive resulted in him ultimately becoming lucky. He had not always been lucky in life, though: as a child he dreamed of becoming a musician or soldier, but was forced to relinquish those dreams after contracting polio in his early teens. Then, while in his sickbed, Koshiba encountered physics when his teacher sent him *The Evolution of Physics* by Albert Einstein and Leopold Infeld, which set him on the path to winning a Nobel Prize decades later.

Koichi Tanaka also had a setback when he was

Lucky People

applying for jobs and his application was rejected by the home appliance manufacturer that was his first choice. Instead, he was accepted by the Shimadzu Corporation, where he had applied to the medical instruments department, since he wanted to work in an area beneficial to human health. Initially disappointed at being assigned to the company's central research laboratory instead, his research there eventually led to winning a Nobel Prize. This kind of thing happens all the time: events that initially seem unwelcome or negative later turn out to be something positive.

People who are often singled out as lucky have frequently had bad experiences, setbacks and disappointments in their past. What they all have in common is never losing hope when bad things happen. Naturally – like all of us – they suffer, become down-cast, have regrets, and even feel totally devastated, but they do not give in to despair. They don't become petulant and throw things around. They take on board unwelcome developments, accept them, then they shift gears and ask themselves, 'OK, what can I do?' In contrast, when unwelcome things happen to unlucky people, they become overly fixated on it. 'What a disaster, it's

"People who are often singled out as lucky have frequently had bad experiences, setbacks and disappointments in their past."

hopeless,' they say to themselves, and fall into despair. They are prone to wanting to throw everything away.

'Bad experiences' is a phrase that could cover a multitude of situations – from major blows to minor wounds – but most such experiences can be categorised as occasional upsets or short-term concerns, and so, if something negative does occur, don't dwell on the outcome too much. Instead, accept that this is how things are for the time being, rather than struggling against a negative outcome. This may not be easy, but you should at least try. Then you can move on and think about how to make the most of the situation. Anyone who can do this can be called a lucky person.

Lucky People Always Have Their Dreams in Mind

Imagine you won the jackpot in the lottery. Other than saving it, what would you do with the money? Are you able to answer the question without hesitating? If so, you can call yourself a lucky person, because knowing what you want is key to realising your dreams and grasping any opportunities that come your way.

Lucky People Set Their Own Standards for Happiness

People who can do this, or have serendipitous experiences, are able to do so because they always have their dreams or goals in mind. They are always thinking about them and picturing themselves having achieved them. Often, our goals or dreams are not the kind of thing that money can buy, but in many cases money can be a useful means of getting to them. When an unexpected windfall comes their way, anyone who is always thinking about their dream will know instantly how they could make use of it and is a lucky person.

It is the same principle as wishing upon a falling star. It is not the star that will make your dreams come true, but being in a state of always having those dreams in mind which brings you closer to achieving them. So try to be clear in your mind what these are for you, remembering the importance of making sure they align with your own standards for happiness. Check that they are indeed your own goals, and you are not simply taking on other people's expectations or opinions.

Another important point is to make sure your goals are realistic. The brain will react against anything too unrealistic, stymying you from becoming sufficiently motivated or enthusiastic. If your aspirations are

Lucky People

too high, try scaling them down to something more achievable. A history enthusiast might want to travel back in time to a particular period in history, which is totally unrealistic, but they could eat the same kind of diet as in that period or surround themselves with literature from that time.

It is also important not to confuse the means with the goal. Wishing to win the lottery, get into the university of your choice, or lose more weight might typically be considered as wishes, but in fact they are not. Money, education and looks are nothing more than the means of achieving goals and making dreams come true; it is what comes after these things that you ought to think about. What is the point of winning the lottery? Why do you want to get into a particular university? Why do you want to be slimmer? This is what you must be clear about.

Once you are clear about your goals and dreams, always be conscious of them. The brain is forgetful, which is why writing hopes and dreams down on paper is effective. You often hear this recommended as a way of helping to make your goals come true, but another method is to pin up a photo or picture of your goal.

Lucky People Set Their Own Standards for Happiness

Here, the neurotransmitter dopamine – which we know is secreted when humans feel joy or happiness – plays a part. When you stare at a piece of paper with your hopes and dreams written on it, or at a photo of something you desire, the brain naturally creates an image of you achieving that goal or obtaining the desired object. For example, if you are flicking through a fashion magazine while thinking that you want some new clothes, and you come across a page with photos of clothes that appeal to you, your heart will give a little leap in reaction. This is the result of the brain feeling joy at imagining what it would be like to actually own those clothes. These moments of anticipation at receiving a reward are what cause the brain to feel pleasure. This pleasure can be even greater in intensity than when you actually get the reward, and it is what motivates people to move to action. The same thing happens when we see our goals or dreams written down on paper: the brain imagines what it would be like to achieve these and feels pleasure, triggering the release of dopamine. Dopamine motivates and spurs us on to take the action that will lead to achieving our goals.

Write your dreams and goals down on paper, look at

Lucky People

it often, gazing at it until you can picture yourself having achieved them, even when you are not looking at the paper. Then you can feel comfortable that one day, when you suddenly win the lottery, you'll already know exactly what to do with the money.

Chapter Five

Lucky People Pray

Lucky People Say Positive Prayers

Put concrete effort and inventiveness aside for the moment, and just pray. This needn't be a religious prayer or directed at a specific god. It could be a prayer to your ancestors, providence or a guardian spirit, but wherever it is that you choose to focus your thoughts on, put your hands together and pray for your dreams to come true and your luck to improve.

I believe it is good to make time to do this. Praying can have a positive effect on mental and physical health, and by extension be conducive to enhancing your luck. You might ask what kind of prayers can have a positive influence like this; the answer is the kind that express your wish for the happiness of someone else as well as yourself.

For example, on their customary new year visit to a shrine, many Japanese business people are likely to pray for better business results in the coming year.

" Praying can have a positive effect on mental and physical health, and by extension be conducive to enhancing your luck."

Such prayers focused solely on individual happiness could be reframed by taking into consideration who else would benefit if personal business performance were improved. Perhaps that person would get a raise if this happened and be able to take their family on a holiday they've long dreamed about. Perhaps the person praying markets a good-quality product and, instead of thinking about their own financial gain from it, could try to picture all the people who will benefit from the convenience and enjoyment of that product.

Single people in search of a partner could pray to meet someone who also makes their parents happy, rather than simply someone nice. Young parents might pray to find a home where children can grow up in freedom and comfort, and friends and family can come to stay. Think of the bigger picture, of what lies beyond the specific thing you want to come true, and how others' happiness is involved in that, then make this the focus of your prayer.

We have already seen that the medial prefrontal cortex plays a role in assessing our individual actions. This part of the brain also passes judgement on prayers, and naturally it deems a prayer for someone else's happiness much better than one solely for our own benefit. Negative prayers – such as wanting to get the better of another person, or wanting them to fail – will be judged by the self as 'bad prayers'.

When the brain judges a prayer as good, it releases pleasure hormones. This is the general term for neurotransmitters such as beta-endorphin, dopamine and oxytocin that cause feel-good emotions and sensations. Of these, beta-endorphin works to activate the brain, raising immunity and preventing various illnesses. The release of beta-endorphin is also known for improving memory and concentration. Oxytocin is also believed to boost memory. By contrast, a prayer that the brain judges to be 'bad' will trigger release of the stress chemical cortisol. Cortisol is essential for life but overproduction of it is known to cause atrophy of the hippocampus, which plays a central role in the brain's memory circuit. In this way, 'good prayers' have a positive effect on physical and mental health, while 'bad prayers' have a negative impact.

That said, I do not recommend overdoing it when you think about the happiness of others. The medial prefrontal cortex is a harsh judge and will see through any

"Think of the bigger picture, of what lies beyond the specific thing you want to come true, and how others' happiness is involved in that, then make this the focus of your prayer."

lies. It recognises any insincerities tacked on to a prayer as hypocritical, and won't judge them as positive prayer. So never force yourself, but still try to think about the happiness of people other than yourself in your prayers. It will have a beneficial effect on your mind and body, in turn making your wishes more easily realised.

Lucky People Pray for Many Others

Wishes will be fulfilled more easily when you think of and pray for the happiness of many people rather than just yourself.

Let's say your prayer is to save more money. Such a prayer is not completely futile as it can be motivating and give you a goal, but simply praying for it won't increase your savings; it depends on the actions you take after praying to save more money.

This is where differences can be seen between those who think only of their own happiness and those who have others' happiness in sight. The differences in their conduct is most apparent in difficult situations. Say, for example, you want to save money but the company where you work has just folded. It's a small business

"Wishes will be fulfilled more easily when you think of and pray for the happiness of many people rather than just yourself."

and everybody must leave. In such a situation, anyone whose aim is to save money only for their own benefit will easily give up on their goal. They are likely to assume that it is impossible under the circumstances, limit themselves to saving enough to eat, and abandon their goal. However, anyone whose aim is to make and save money for the benefit of others, such as family, friends or staff, does not give up so easily. They are resourceful and will rack their brains to come up with an idea or plan to help them. They make a big effort.

In his book *Ketsudan no keiei* (The management of decision-making), Panasonic founder Kōnosuke Matsushita wrote, 'whenever I was making impossible demands during negotiations with customers, I kept a picture of my hard-working employees in my head.' As company manager, Matsushita sometimes needed to make difficult requests from his business contacts – things that were of little benefit to the other party in the short term, but without which Matsushita's own company could not keep going. At such times he would think of his employees' faces. If he were asking just for himself, it would have been easy to scale down the request and be done with it. But behind him were several hundred employees, whose hard efforts working for him would have been in vain, so he could not back down. He was not trying to make money just for his own benefit, but for his employees as well.

It works that way in many situations: I am more motivated to cook when there is someone to share a meal with, rather than cooking only for myself, and it is easier to stick to a diet when there is somebody else to celebrate weight-loss wins with. Doing something solely for your own benefit doesn't trigger any big changes in the brain, but if you do something for someone else's benefit your brain recognises this action as 'good behaviour' and releases feel-good chemicals, so we feel more comfortable doing something for someone else rather than just for ourselves. The more people who benefit from our actions, the greater the level of feel-good chemicals released by the brain.

We are more able to persevere and try much harder when we do something for someone else's benefit rather than simply for ourselves. So, when praying for something, try to include more people in your thoughts. This is also one secret to making your wishes come true more easily.

" We are more able to persevere and try much harder when we do something for someone else's benefit rather than simply for ourselves."

Lucky People Pray for the Happiness of Their Enemies

In your prayers, think of someone other than yourself, and wish for the happiness of as many people as possible. If you can do this, the next challenge is to pray for the happiness of your enemies.

Is there someone in your life you dislike or find difficult to interact with? Deciding not to give them a single thought is one method of dealing with such people, but annoyingly they tend to occupy our minds with surprising frequency. Thinking about people we dislike causes the brain to release the stress chemical cortisol. As we know, cortisol is an essential hormone for life, but too much of it affects the body adversely by raising blood pressure and sugar levels, lowering immunity, and affecting memory and mental health. Instead, if you can pray for the happiness of people you dislike, the brain will release feel-good chemicals that have a favourable effect on the body and mind. That said, it is not easy to have a complete change of heart about someone you can't stand.

We all have times when all we can think about is

somebody we dislike. When this happens to me, I try to take inspiration from the Gautama Siddhartha Buddha and the way he dealt with his cousin Devadatta. Devadatta was talented but very envious of Gautama. He tried to kill Gautama several times, and led 500 of Gautama's followers away in a breakaway religious group. He was the epitome of an enemy for Gautama. But according to the record in the *Lotus Sutra*, Gautama declared that Devadatta had been his holy teacher in a past life and would attain Buddhahood in a future life.

The Dalai Lama XIV and his campaigning for the freedom and democracy of Tibet provides another inspiring model. Along with the people of Tibet, he has been subject to severe oppression from the Chinese government. Yet he has made statements to the effect that he does not hold hatred for the Chinese people themselves, and said that 'your enemies are your best spiritual teachers because their presence provides you with the opportunity to enhance and develop tolerance, patience and understanding.' For most of us it would be difficult to reach the enlightened state of Buddha or the Dalai Lama, but it is possible to try to move closer to their attitudes and examples.

By taking a calm view of things, many of the people we dislike serve as examples we can learn from. Sometimes it leads to the discovery that what we dislike most about them is also in ourselves, and this becomes a chance to rectify those things. By making the effort to think in this way, your perception of and attitude to the people you find difficult or unlikable may start to change a little. This doesn't mean suddenly forcing yourself to pray for the happiness of people you hate – the brain will see through any such attempt as a lie – but you can work on changing your view of people you dislike, little by little. By doing this, your brain should also change for the better.

Lucky People Pray for the Sick

When a friend or family member falls ill, we naturally wish them a quick recovery. This is an example of a prayer that is all about the other person, and I truly believe it can be effective to at least some degree.

You have probably heard of the placebo effect. A placebo in medicine is a pill that appears exactly like the real thing but is made of sugar and contains no

"Sometimes it leads to the discovery that what we dislike most about them is also in ourselves, and this becomes a chance to rectify those things."

effective ingredients. Placebos are used to confirm the efficacy of new drugs during trials that compare subjects who take the new drug with those who take the placebo. Subjects taking the placebo do not know, and believe they are taking the real drug. In about 30 per cent of cases, subjects given the placebo experience the effects of the medicine even though it ought not to be possible. This means approximately one in three people experience actual effects of the medicine, just through believing it will work.

In an experiment conducted by psychiatrists Lee Park and Lino Covi, patients were given pills that they were told contained only sugar, but that other patients with the same condition had been helped by such pills after taking them for three weeks. Approximately one third of subjects felt an effect when none should have been possible. Even when the person knew they were taking a placebo, their belief in the doctor's words had an effect.

Another interesting phenomenon is the nocebo effect: when a patient believes in the harmful quality of a substance that is not actually medically harmful, and this contributes to illness or death. We see this when a

Lucky People

patient is given a drug and told there is a possibility of it causing certain symptoms, and those symptoms then occur even though the medicine was a placebo. Or when a patient who has been continually taking a specific medication strongly believes in its efficacy but becomes convinced that the doctor stopped administering the medicine, and then that medication ceases to be effective even if it is still actually being administered.

The placebo and nocebo effects both go to show that even changes affecting life and death can occur in the body just through the power of belief. The more strongly a person believes, the higher the likelihood there is some kind of change occurring.

When a person knows they are the recipient of good wishes and prayers from others, it reinforces the strength of this belief. Say somebody has fallen seriously ill. That person may think they don't have much time left, but still has a strong desire to live and a faint hope of being able to pull through. Seeing this, their family prays desperately. The person sees their family praying and in response thinks they must do their best to stay alive for their loved ones. They realise there is meaning in staying alive, and this realisation can help them find the strength to keep living. In some cases, the family's optimistic mindset and their prayers can be transferred to the patient through the agency of mirror neurons. There are also cases when the brain's reward system is stimulated in the person who found meaning in being alive, activating immune cells such as natural killer cells and helping to heal the illness.

Prayer from the heart can effect change in others' bodies. Of course, it cannot be said that prayer alone will cure all illnesses completely, but, on occasion, prayer can work to aid in healing. This is a fact worth believing in.

"In some cases, the family's optimistic mindset and their prayers can be transferred to the patient through the agency of mirror neurons."

Epilogue

Lucky People Cultivate a Lucky Brain

I believe cultivating a 'lucky brain' is a good way to start improving your luck.

We have already considered the mindset, behavioural patterns and conduct that lucky people have in common. We know that luck is not innate or something we are born with, and that it can change according to mindset and patterns of behaviour we adopt. So the place to start making changes is the brain itself, as that is what determines a person's thoughts and actions. In other words, we should cultivate a lucky brain.

It was once believed that brain cells began to decrease in number after we reach maturity, never to increase again, and that each individual brain is determined by genes, like a blueprint, and fixed in accordance with this blueprint once we reach adulthood. However, in 1998 Swedish scientist Peter Eriksson and American neuroscientist Fred Gage discovered that new synapses (the junctions between nerve cells) could be generated in the adult brain. They examined the brain of hospitalised patients after death and found that neurogenesis had been occurring in the dentate gyrus of the hippocampus (a part of the brain's temporal lobe that is critical for memory encoding and retrieval). We now also know that the brain is continually changing through new experiences that provide it with new stimulation. This is known as brain plasticity and it means that our brains can continue to grow, no matter how old we are.

So how do we change the brain? And how can we turn our brains into lucky brains? One method is prayer. In the previous chapter, we saw the positive impact that good prayers can have on the brain. Even praying once can have a definite beneficial effect on the brain if the prayer is a good one and from the heart. However, if you are hoping to change daily behaviour and attitudes, just one prayer will have no effect.

Cells in the human body are believed to take about three months to replace. In the case of hard systems like the skeleton, it can take longer, but for skin and muscle it is about three months. As most of the brain is composed of fat, brain cells too are believed to take about three months to be replaced. This is why praying needs to become a regular habit to effect change in the brain.

Lucky People Cultivate a Lucky Brain

I would like to recommend methodically praying twice a day, morning and night. Making the time to examine and compose yourself at the beginning and end of each day, as a means of developing your brain, is the most worthwhile thing you can do. This works even better in conjunction with going to bed early, rising early and getting enough sleep. Praying in the morning sunlight promotes the release of serotonin, the hormone that promotes mood stabilisation. And since it is easier to have an optimistic attitude in the morning rather than at night, use the mornings to focus on forward-looking thoughts, such as the self you want to be in future or the goals you want to achieve. Recent studies have shown there is increased activity in the hippocampus when humans vividly visualise the future. The hippocampus plays a central role in the memory circuit, which means that praying on the morning of exams may also be effective.

Night-time is a chance to look back on the day and reflect: what did you do that contributed to your future self and goals? What were you not able to do? And what can you do tomorrow?

The habit of daily prayer is also a useful way of

keeping goals and dreams in the forefront of your mind so as to make them more achievable.

Be aware, however, that the brain is apt to form mechanical routines and patterns out of an inherent desire to increase the number of processes that can be done 'without thinking about it'. The act of prayer is also susceptible to this tendency, so it is easy to fall into the trap of simply praying through habit, in which case the resulting 'prayer by rote' will have no beneficial effect on the brain. Hence it is important to always be mindful when praying. To do this, it helps to have a predetermined physical position, time and place for your prayers. Decide where and how you will do it – perhaps you can do your morning prayers sitting in the sun immediately after getting up, and your evening prayers while sitting cross-legged and composing yourself before bed. Then, every day, morning and evening, offer up heartfelt prayer. If you can continue with this, the brain will succeed in achieving positive change and become a 'lucky brain'.

The various methods I have laid out in this book to improve your luck are available to anybody. I hope that in some small way they can help you lead a happy life and be a lucky person.

References

BOOKS

Nadine de Rothschild, *Le bonheur de séduire, l'art de réussir* [The Happiness of Seducing, the Art of Succeeding] (Japanese edition translated by Hisako Ito, 1993, Kobunsha)

Albert Einstein and Leopold Infeld, *The Evolution of Physics* (Japanese edition translated by Jun Ishihara, Iwanami Shoten, 2008)

Katherine Ellison, *The Mommy Brain: How Motherhood Makes You Smarter* (Japanese edition translated by Mioko Nishida, published by SB Creative, 2005)

Satoshi Fujii, *Naze shojikimonoha toku wo surunoka* [Why honest people reap rewards] (Gentosha, 2009)

Kōnosuke Matsushita, *Ketsudan no keiei* [The manage-ment of decision-making] (PHP Institute Inc., 1979)

Kazuo Murakami, *Kiseki wo yobu 100 mankai no inori* [A million prayers bring miracles] (SB Creative, 2011)

Lucky People

Robert F. Kroeger, *Lifenuts: A Community-Based Blueprint for Individuals to Live Longer, Healthier, and Happier* (Xlibris, 2012)

Koichi Tanaka, *Shogai saiko no shippai* [Life's best mistakes] (Asahi Shimbun Co., 2003)

ARTICLES

D. R. Addis, D. L. Schacter, 'The hippocampus and imagining the future: where do we stand?', *Front Hum Neurosci*, National Library of Medicine, 2012, https://pmc.ncbi.nlm.nih.gov/articles/PMC3251274/

J. C. Croizet, G. Després, M. E. Gauzins, P. Huguet, J. P. Leyens and A. Méot, 'Stereotype threat undermines intellectual performance by triggering a disruptive mental load', *Pers Soc Psychol Bull*, National Library of Medicine, 2004, https://pubmed.ncbi.nlm.nih.gov/15155036/#:~:text=Abstract,actual%20differences%20in%20cognitive%20ability

Satoshi Fujii, '解明！ 運がない人は、なぜ運がないのか' ['Explained! Why are unlucky people unlucky?'], 15 August 2011, President.jp, https://president.jp/articles/-/8829?page=1

Akiko Ikeda (Akiko Nakagami), 'マーモセットの父親のホルモンレベルと養育行動に関する研究' ['Hormone levels and parenting behaviour in marmosets fathers'], National Center of Neurology and Psychiatry, Kaken, 2014, https://kaken.nii.ac.jp/ja/grant/KAKENHI-PROJECT-24600020/

References

Timothy A. Judge and Charlice Hurst, 'How the rich (and happy) get richer (and happier): Relationship of core self-evaluations to trajectories in attaining work success', University of Florida, *Journal of Applied Psychology*, American Psychological Association, 2008, Vol. 93, No. 4, pp. 849–863.

William D. Lassek, Steven J.C. Gaulin, 'Waist-hip ratio and cognitive ability: is gluteofemoral fat a privileged store of neurodevelopmental resources?', *Evolution and Human Behavior*, Vol. 29, Issue 1, 2008, pp. 26–34, https://www.sciencedirect.com/science/article/abs/pii/S1090513807000736

Hideki Matsui et al., 'オキシトシンによる扁桃体機能のモジュレーションと情動の制御' ['Modulating amygdala functions and regulating emotions with oxytocin'], Okayama University, Kaken, 2006, https://kaken.nii.ac.jp/ja/grant/KAKENHI-PROJECT-17300127/

Tetsuya Ohira, quoted in: '毎日たくさん笑って、将来の認知症リスクを低くしよう！' ['Laugh a lot every day and reduce your risk of dementia in the future!'], angfa.jp, 11 December 2012, https://www.angfa.jp/karada-aging/practice/sonota28/

Lee Park and Lino Covi, 'Nonblind Placebo Trial: An Exploration of Neurotic Patients' Responses to Placebo When Its Inert Content Is Disclosed', *Arch Gen Psychiatry*, Jama Netwok, 1965, pp. 336–345, https://jamanetwork.com/journals/jamapsychiatry/article-abstract/488749

G. Rizzolatti and L. Craighero, 'Mirror neuron: a neurological approach to empathy', in: J. P. Changeux, A. R. Damasio, W. Singer, Y. Christen (eds), *Neurobiology of Human Values, Research (Perspectives in Neurosciences)*, Springer, 2005, pp. 107–123, https://link.springer.com/chapter/10.1007/3-540-29803-7_9#citeas

Norihiro Sadato et al., 'Processing of Social and Monetary Rewards in the Human Striatum', *Neuron*, Elsevier, Vol. 58, Issue 2, 2008, pp. 284–294.

Science Editor & Steve Connor, 'The myth of female intuition exploded by fake smile test', *Independent*, 12 April 2005, https://www.independent.co.uk/news/science/the-myth-of-female-intuition-exploded-by-fake-smile-test-484585.html

Erin Faith Thompson, 'Relationship of women's hip anthropometrics with aerobic fitness and attractiveness', Stephen F. Austin State University, 2015.

'ブラック企業就職偏差値ランキング' ['Black Company Employment Standard Deviation Ranking'], Yourpedia, https://ja.yourpedia.org/wiki/%E3%83%96%E3%83%A9%E3%83%83%E3%82%AF%E4%BC%81%E6%A5%AD%E5%B0%B1%E8%81%B7%E5%81%8F%E5%B7%AE%E5%80%A4%E3%83%A9%E3%83%B3%E3%82%AD%E3%83%B3%E3%82%B0

'大阪発 笑いのススメ' ['Promoting laughter from Osaka'], Osaka Prefecture Department of Citizens' Life and Culture, March 2016, p. 6, https://www.pref.osaka.lg.jp/documents/85311/waraisasshi.pdf

About the Author

NOBUKO NAKANO was born in Tokyo. In 2008, she received a PhD in neuroscience from the Tokyo University Graduate School of Medicine. She is a specially appointed Professor at Higashi Nippon International University, and sits on the Board of Trustees at Mori Art Museum. She has studied and written extensively on the brain and psychology. Her publications include: *How to Vomit Up Poison Elegantly: What neuroscience and Kyotoyites can teach us about the art of conveying difficult truths* (Nikkei BP, 2023); *Darkness of the Brain* (Shinchosha, 2023); *Psychopath* (Bungei Shunju, 2016); *Habits of Smart People Around the World Collected in One Volume* (Ascom Inc., 2021); *Toxic Parents* (Poplar, 2020) and *Fake* (Shogakukan, 2022).